I0140928

Dressage Training
for Professional Horse Lovers

by
Prof. Dr. Konstanze Krueger
and Knut Krueger

Translation from the German by Elisabeth D'Antoni

© 2014 Xenophon Verlag e. K
All rights reserved.
ISBN-13: 978-3-9808134-64

Dressage Training for Professional Horse Lovers

A scientific approach to dressage training
that emphasizes the horse's physical and mental well-being

X

© 2014 www.xenophon-publishing.com

Table of Contents

Introduction

Introduction

"Training: The purpose of training is to prepare horses for tests in such a way that they are in peak physiological and mental condition at the start, and that they can pass the tests at full performance capacity without damage to their trust, health or nerves."
Richtlinien für Reiten und Fahren Band II Kapitel III (2001)

"Ultimately it has been established that one of the major tasks of every training session should be to create a relationship of trust between the horse and the rider. Only in this way will an eager, competitive team develop that will be able to cope respectably with the diverse situations presented by any three-day event."
Richtlinien für Reiten und Fahren Band II Kapitel III (2001)

Both of these quotes were taken from the book Richtlinien für Reiten und Fahren Band II Kapitel III "Richtlinien für die Viel-seitigkeitsausbildung" (2001) (Guidelines for Riding and Driving Vol. II, Chapter III "Guidelines for training for three-day events"). In all of the literature pertaining to riding, references to training methods seem to apply exclusively to endurance sports like three-day eventing, endurance riding and sometimes for jumping and racing.

Sufficient explanations about how to apply specific training methods to the dressage horse are nowhere to be found, even though the above-mentioned quotes are just as applicable to the sport of dressage as they are to endurance sports. It should be mentioned at this juncture that, in fact, dressage is the basis for any equine training. In this regard, as in many others, we agree completely with Philippe Karl (2006), who points out explicitly that all riders, no matter what style of riding or type of equestrian sport they are involved in, are obliged to train their horses in dressage to some extent, whether they are aware of it or not. After all, the goal of dressage is to train the horse's balance, suppleness, agility, reaction speed, as well as strength and stamina, while carrying a rider.

Awareness of the effects that training stimuli have on muscle function and the cardiovascular system is of crucial importance for the understanding of proper training. For this reason, the following pages will examine the latest information available about training methods, the theoretical background of anatomy, physiology and rehabilitation training in human high performance sports. We will explain this theoretical background more precisely as it pertains to the training of the dressage horse, and then finally we will give specific instructions and tips for the rider and trainer in order to implement these theories in the daily training of dressage horses.

Since it is pointless to use brilliant training methods if they don't fit harmoniously into the overall training strategy, we consider it of utmost importance to present a variety of training alternatives for the basic training of diverse movements in dressage. A dressage horse does not have to do moderate dressage work in a covered riding hall seven days a week. What is crucial in turning the horse and rider into an "eager competitive team" as we mentioned before is a comprehensive, varied and flexible training program. Diverse exercises in the dressage ring, over small jumps, on the racetrack and out on the trail will keep your equine partner healthy and contented, while strengthening his nerves. Even the "leisure time" of a dressage horse spent grazing in a pasture and trail riding can be used, on the one hand, for his mental recuperation and on the other hand for the gentle development of his physical strength. In this book we are expressly giving you tips on how you can train your dressage horse for high performance in a diverse and profit-able way, while carefully protecting his mind and body, in all of the training disciplines available.

In the last chapter a few dressage lessons will be selected and presented according to our training methods. However, we won't provide any exact instructions about giving the horse aids for the different dressage movements. So much has been written on this topic in so many outstanding riding instruction books that we don't want to add to that list. Instead, in this book we want to concentrate on the special aspects of training for dressage horses.

Of course, the training options discussed here are by no means complete. They come from classical riding, our own experience and as a comparison to training in human high-performance sports. Certainly numerous trainers have achieved good results using other methods. A discussion of the different training methods in equestrian sports would be highly recommended in the future.

Further references:

Karl Philippe. Twisted Truths of Modern Dressage: The Search for the Classic Alternative. (Brunsbek: Cadmus Verlag, 2007)

Guidelines for Riding and Driving. Vol. 1, 'Basic training for rider and horse', (Warendorf: FN Verlag, 2008, 2013).

Guidelines for Riding and Driving. Vol. 2, 'Advanced training', (Warendorf: FN Verlag, 2001).

Short digression to look at history

It is interesting to note that the study of equine training methods is a young science. If you think about how dependent man and horse were on the performance of their bodies over the past centuries, this is truly astonishing. Generally, strength, stamina, speed and health were seen as gifts from God. Either you had them or you didn't.

However, there are a few reports that reach us from antiquity about individuals who increased their strength through specific training programs. For example, there is a little anecdote about Milon from Croton 550-510 B.C. (Umminger, 1962):

Milon can still be regarded as one of the most successful Olympians of all times. For thirty years he dominated Olympic wrestling without ever being defeated. However, as a child he was a weakling and was constantly teased by the other children in the neighborhood. One day he decided to put an end to the teasing. He took a calf from his father's stable and carried it around the house several times. In the beginning this was very difficult for him, but as the calf grew, so did his strength. In the end he was able to carry a full-grown bull. Milon's strength was admired everywhere. Oddly enough, it apparently never occurred to anyone to duplicate his training method, nor did anyone learn a lesson from his steady increase of strength.

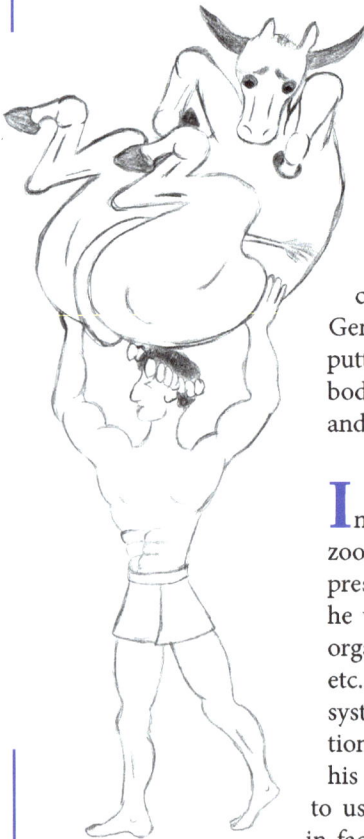

Yet the word "training" was used rather early on, especially in England in the context of equine sports. But, up into the 20th century, the body's ability to perform was regarded as something genetic, even mysterious, which should be treated cautiously and used sparingly. Generally people were convinced that putting too much of a strain on the body would lead to premature wear and tear.

In 1809 in his book Philosophie zoologique, for the first time Lamarck presented the theory that organs, and he wasn't only referring to the inner organs such as the heart, lungs, liver, etc., but also to the biomechanical system, could be trained in proportion to the amount they were used. In his opinion, the more organs were put to use, the stronger they became, and in fact the lack of use could even lead to complete atrophy. Even Steinbrecht (*1808, †1885) claimed in many parts

Milon from Croton

of his book Gymnasium des Pferdes (Exercising of the Horse), published by Plinzner, that strengthening and exercising dressage horses made sense. He forcefully pointed out that, since it was rare for the professional rider to have exceptionally talented dressage horses available to him, it would be necessary to take average horses and, with the proper training program, turn them into good, useful horses.

Steinbrecht was far ahead of his time with these demands. Unfortunately, these thoughts, which were quite progressive at the time, disappeared from people's minds for about 150 years. Darwin, with his thesis about the "Survival of the Fittest", revolutionized scientific thought in Europe in the middle of the 19th C. These insights from Darwin, which were very important on the one hand, had an unfortunate stagnating effect on the development of training programs. Very strict Darwinian principles about inherited genetic characteristics and performance produced the fatalistic attitude toward sports during the previous centuries.

It wasn't until the beginning of the 20th C that Lamarck's theory was taken up once again. In 1914 in an athletic yearbook, a gymnastics instructor named Sturm, from Tübingen University referred to, among other things, Lamarck's statement that "function makes the organ". In the same year the physiologist Du Bois-Reymond published an article clearly supporting the principle that performance can be improved through training. However, he neglected to include any advice about what methods should be used to put his theory into practice. Yet already in 1930 Pikhala wrote a full explanation about the principles of training in an athletic yearbook published by Krümmel. The old "wear and tear model" was finally replaced by a new "model for the development and optimization" of physical performance.

Gustav Steinbrecht

A little later the physiologist Cannon (1932) left his mark with the principle of homeostasis. According to this principle, the body is constantly making an effort to develop a flexible balance between its performance and the demands of the environment. If this balance is disturbed, the body temporarily goes into heterostasis and tries to recover a new balance by means of positive feedback.

What can be derived from this principle for training programs is that, for example, higher tension in the muscles promotes growth of the same muscles, and frequent oxygen debt leads to a growth of anaerobic capacity. In an inversion of the argument, muscles waste away without tension, and without cardiac stimulation, the cardiovascular system atrophies. Thus this principle became the foundation for the science of training programs. As time went by, numerous authors published books full of training models and training experience for individual sports.

Soon the new insights into training programs started to be used in endurance sports such as eventing and long-distance riding. Klimke (1967) reported on his own experiences with the "new" training programs in his book Military (Eventing). In 1980 Karstens introduced different forms of conditioning for eventing. A collection of authors wrote down their opinions about training and competitive programs that were published by Oese in 1982. However, practical parallels to the theoretical basics mainly included eventing and jumping. In the chapter about dressage training, the authors spent most of their time describing the various dressage movements in detail, yet direct advice about general fitness training for the dressage horse was completely missing, as well as how this training might relate to the special demands of the sport.

Leng (1990) also integrated the training of the dressage horse into the training of the event horse. Although event riders don't pursue the sport of dressage for its own sake, but rather primarily for the effect it has on the gymnastic ability and increased rideability of the horse, in this section event riders found many useful tips on how to influence the basic gaits and how to perform dressage movements. Of course, event riders avoid doing any planned, specific dressage training, since the resulting increase in muscle size would work against the aerobic endurance required of the event horse.

Sprigorum wrote what is possibly one of the most comprehensive publications about the application of training programs in equestrian sports in 1986. It is called Hinweis zum Konditionstraining der Military-Pferde (Advice for Conditioning Event Horses), which is

Charles Darwin

Jean-Baptiste de Lamarck

strictly for event riders and horses. However, the fundamentals discussed in this book can also be applied to the dressage horse.

Christine Heipertz-Hengst (1999), Kerstin Diacont / Andrea Löffler (2010) and Renate Ettl (2007,2008) published a broad spectrum of training tips for all areas of equestrian sports.

A review of the important points:

• The use of training methods is a young science.

• Lamarck laid the foundations for training methods with his theories about the development of organs by increased use.

• Numerous training methods have been published for eventing and endurance sports, which can only be applied to dressage to a certain extent, since dressage requires a great deal more strength training than any other area of equestrian sports.

• In particular, interval training in human sports can be applied to the training methods for dressage.

Further references:

Darwin, Charles. The foundation of the origin of species. (London: Cambridge University Press, 1842).

Ettl, R. Pferde gut in Form - Richtiges Training für Fitness und Gesundheit. (Stuttgart: Müller-Rüschlikon, 2007).

Ettl, R. Horse-Agility - Spielerisch und anspruchsvoll trainieren. (Stuttgart: Müller Rüschlikon, 2008).

Lamarck, J-B. Zoologische Philosophie, Mit Einleitung und Anhang: Das phylogenetische System der Tiere nach Haeckel. (Leipzig: Kröner, 1909).

Springorum, B. Hinweise zum Konditionstraining der Military-Pferde. (Warendorf: FN-Verlag, 1986).

Steinbrecht, G. Das Gymnasium des Pferdes. (Berlin: Richard Schröder, 1935).

Diacont, K.; Löffler, A. Richtiges Training - Gesundes Pferd: Anatomisches Grundwissen für Reiter und Ausbilder (Müller Rüschlikon 2010)

Physiological, dynamic position of the body

Body Position

Since the 1980s, many physical therapists (such as List 2004, Opitz 2005) have used the treatment ideas in the theories developed by the neurologist Dr. A. Brügger (1980) as a reference work.

Brügger wondered why, in many cases, symptoms of pain caused by various spinal illnesses couldn't be alleviated surgically. He came to the conclusion that many illnesses of the biomechanical system could not be traced to an illness of the spine, but rather seemed to be coming from a protective mechanism of the brain. When the biomechanical system was being used incorrectly, the brain would set off a protective mechanism that manifested itself in certain pain symptoms. Normally the body reacts protectively and with an intensification of its potential for repair. Yet with chronic incorrect pressure, the mechanisms for repair become severely damaged. At first there are functional disorders, then later there can even be changes to the structure, i.e., degeneration of the muscles, tendons, ligaments, joints, and even bones. In Brügger's opinion, the only way to break this chain or to prevent this from happening is the optimal use of biomechanics. This can only be accomplished by assuming a physiological (normal), dynamic position of the body and practicing balanced movement without stress or incorrect pressure. The degree of pressure certain individual structures can tolerate depends on the amount of training they have had.

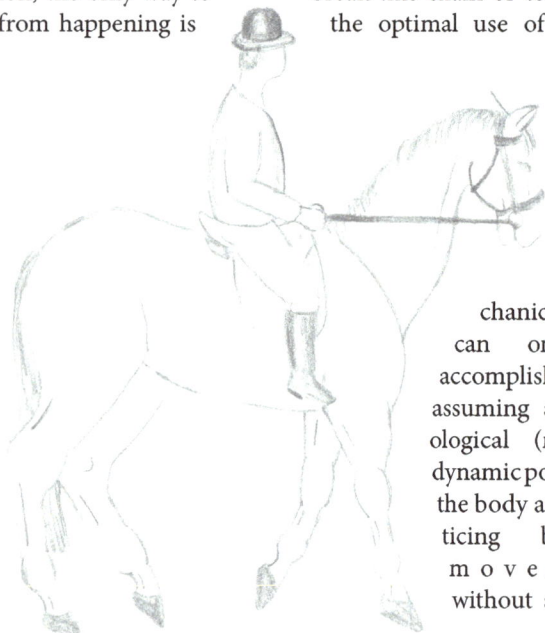

Horse assuming a protective posture to minimize pain

Brügger's theory could also help to avoid problems in the biomechanical system of dressage horses. But what exactly does the physiological, dynamic position of the horse's body look like? The horse spends most of his day at a walk. The position of his body corresponds to a horse walking with a rider when the reins are given completely. More than 60% of his weight is carried by the forehand. The driving power of the hindquarters is hardly used at all. The faster the gait, the more important the hindquarters become, since the dynamic components of the movement's potential are mainly derived from the hind legs. Even in movements without the rider, the horse pushes his weight toward the hindquarters at a trot and even more at a canter. Simultaneously, the horse begins to arch both back and neck. His neck and head no longer hang long and low, but instead they are held up. The higher the horse holds his head up, the closer his noseline approaches an imaginary vertical line. Usually, however, the nose stays a couple of inches in front of this vertical line. Both the shift of the body's center of gravity to the hindquarters and the lifting of the head take place during play and displays of dominance. This increases the strength and agility of the horse.

If you think about the fact that the rider and the saddle sit closer to the forehand than to the hindquarters on the horse's back, then it becomes clear that even a passive rider pushes the balance of the horse's body toward the forehand. Thus the rider forces the horse to carry an unnatural burden on the forehand. If the horse should also push his back downward, then the balance of the horse's weight distribution drastically worsens at the expense of the forehand. This happens because when the horse's back is hanging down, the tension through the neck and back, which essentially enables the horse to carry the rider, is no longer there. The rider's weight can no longer be distributed over the entire support surface and more of a burden is placed on the forehand.

Quite a few riders have noticed that many horses move in a more confined way and less expressively under the saddle than they do moving freely in a pasture. Right at this point is where the moderate use of dressage can help every riding horse. Dressage teaches the horse how to make up for this imbalance by rebuilding his natural elasticity and the dynamics of his biomechanical system. It is astonishing how the basic gaits improve one after the other as the horse ascends through the training stages of suppleness, contact (between hand and mouth), impulsion and straightening the horse's spine

The horse's weight is shifted to the hindquarters naturally during play.

until he reaches the final stage called collection. Even Steinbrecht (1935) writes that perfect suppleness cannot be achieved until the horse masters the collected lateral movements. Even collection on the hindquarters in movements like piaffe, half passes and other collected movements enables the horse to move in a visibly relaxed and dynamic way.

Referring again to Brügger's thoughts, he considers it senseless to force a horse to work in extreme body positions, to say nothing of demanding high performance of him while maintaining those positions. Short-term stretching of the neck or limbs is certainly comfortable for the horse and helps to relax tense muscle groups. However, if you force the horse to take an unnatural position for a longer period of time, he will certainly be forced to assume a protective posture.

Relaxed on the aids

Horses whose heads are constantly pulled toward their chests, for example, try to counter this by escaping with their hindquarters in an upward direction. Tenseness in the back and the upper region of the

Proper collection

neck quickly appear. Finally, after a few weeks, there will be a clearly visible degradation of the muscles in the back and neck, and the accompanying atrophy of the muscles, tendons, ligaments, etc., is an indication of permanent damage to the biomechanical system. Besides the pain that these horses have to suffer, the rider achieves exactly the opposite effect that appropriate training of the horse should have. The horse is less and less able to balance his rider and carry him easily.

The horse behaves in a similar way when he is constantly ridden with position (not to be confused with the old expression "riding in position"). If the horse's head is constantly

pulled to the side, it severely disturbs the horse's balance. The horse tries to counterbalance, so to speak, by stretching his hindquarters in the opposite direction from which his head is being pulled. No wonder the consequences described in the previous paragraph soon set in.

After Brügger's call for balanced movement without putting the wrong pressure or too much pressure on the horse, a new call followed for the basic training of the horse. This should take place over several years in many small steps according to the horse's abilities and determined by a training plan that has been drawn up for each individual horse. The young horse cannot collect himself yet. First he has to learn how to find a new balance with the rider on his back. During this phase, the best way to help your horse is by

Behind the bit

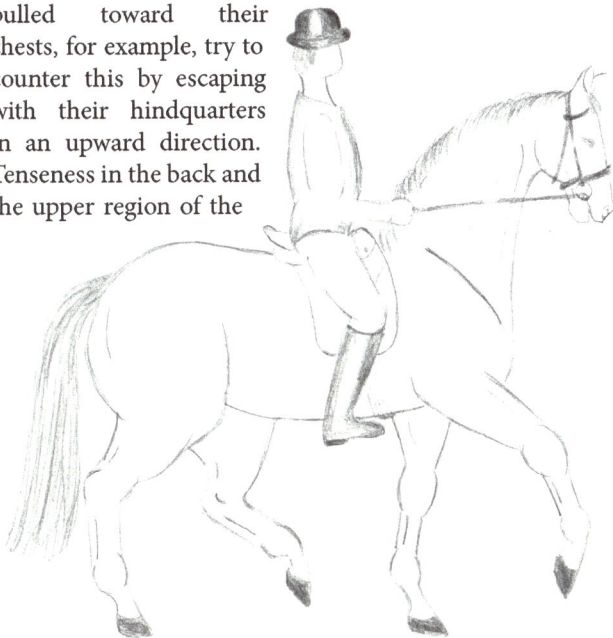

Levade
horse's weight is shifted entirely to the hindquarters

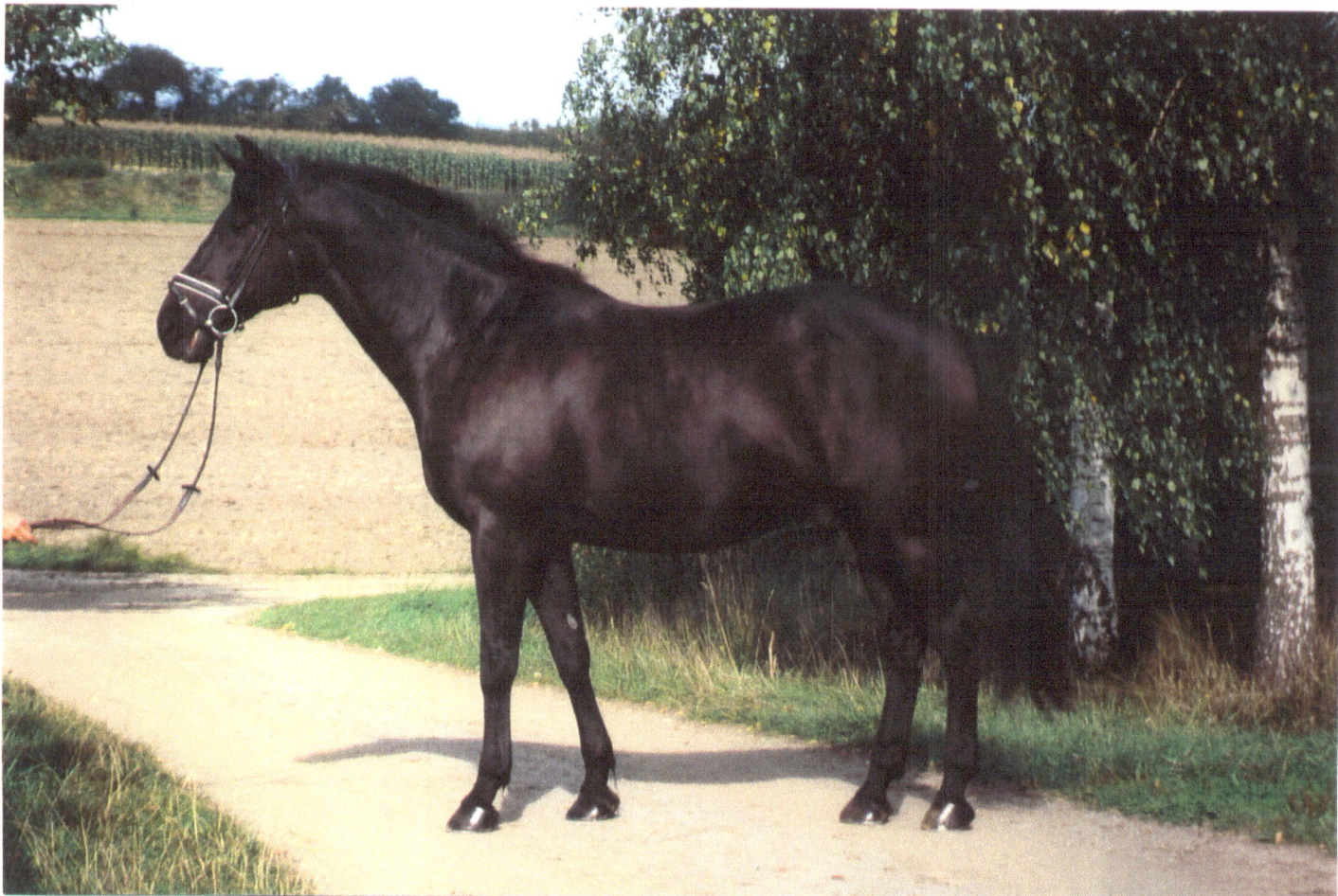

Horse whose basic condition is good

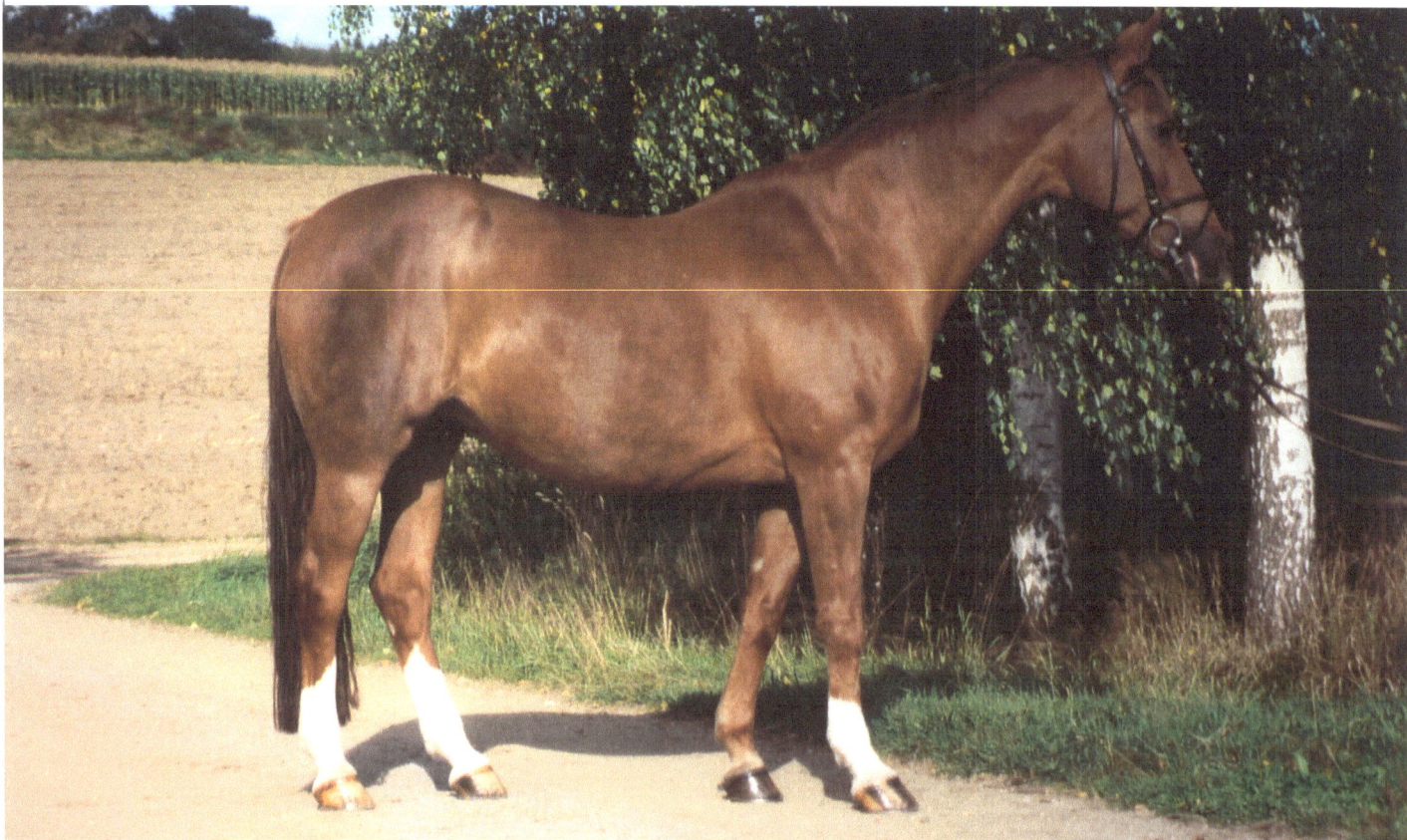

Horse whose basic condition is poor. The pads of fat on her body hide her lack of muscles

showing him "the way into the depths". The horse will quickly realize that with his head carried long and low and his back in a relaxed, raised position, he will be able to carry his rider with ease. It doesn't matter whether it is a young horse that from "one day to the next" has to carry a rider around for hours at a time or an older horse whose basic training hasn't been completed and is suddenly asked for collection over a longer period of time. In both cases the muscles, tendons and especially the joints are hopelessly stressed. As a result, the chain of events Brügger described is triggered and can be expected to conclude with long-term damage to the horse.

The correct basic training and subsequent collection of the horse is precisely what is absolutely necessary for the physiological, dynamic position of the horse that Brügger called for. From this position the horse is able to carry the rider without overburdening the forehand. Riding in the faster gaits without the appropriate training, as well as riding dressage movements on the forehand, are almost the best guarantee that the horse will be damaged as a result.

Since the horse can't tell us when she has reached her limits, the deftness and feeling of both rider and trainer will have to sense this. Basically, the slogan should be "less is more", as always. If you didn't demand very much of your horse on one day, the next day you can demand more. But if you overstrain your horse one day, what usually follows is several days of rest or poor performance.

A review of the important points:

- A physiological, dynamic position of the body is not only important for dressage horses. Every horse should have enough schooling to be able to balance the weight of the rider more easily, which means he can push away from the pressure of the reins and shift his weight to the hindquarters.

- The physiological, dynamic position of the body cannot be forced. It is developed over years of exercising and schooling.

- If some of the steps in training are skipped, the results will be an overburdening of the untrained muscles, tendons, ligaments and joints.

- Using the reins to force the horse into an "upright position" leads to an abnormal posture, since the center of gravity is not being pushed toward the hindquarters. The lack of positive tension in the horse's back caused by this unnatural position will eventually cause damage to the biomechanical system.

- In step-by-step training using the long and low position, horses are able to work in natural collection and hold themselves erect for longer and longer periods of time.

Tips:

- Until the young horse has achieved collection, you should ride him in long, straight lines and avoid narrow turns and circles; otherwise the forehand will be overburdened.

- Ride your young horse low and show her that she can carry the rider more comfortably with her back in a relaxed, slightly raised position.

- Take any signs of exhaustion from your horse seriously in all stages of development. Ask her to repeat the exercise briefly, and then finish the training session.

Further references:

Brügger, A. Gesunde Körperhaltung im Alltag. (Zürich: Dr. A. Brügger, 1980).

List, M. Physiotherapeutische Behandlung in der Traumatologie. (Heidelberg: Springer Verlag, 2004).

Opitz, G. 'Der Muskelschmerz', Schmerz und Akupunktur 3 (2005), 151-163.

Muscles

Muscles are the most important functional unit needed for carrying out a motion sequence. The training of these muscles is the basis for any improvement of performance. Since the understanding of muscle function is extremely important for expedient muscle training, I would like to go into some detail in this chapter about how muscles work.

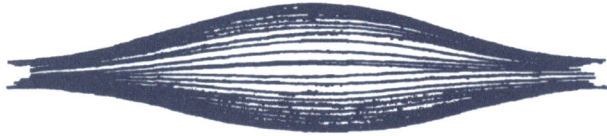

Muscle

Musclefiber

Myofibril

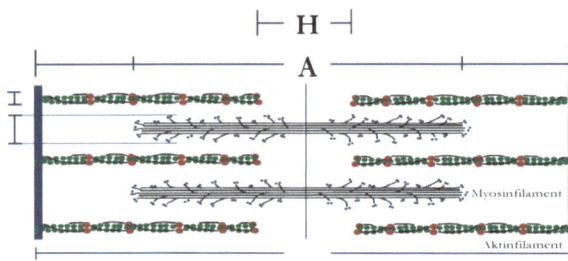

Sarcomere

Composition of a muscle from top to bottom: From the complete muscle down to the smallest functioning unit (modified from A. Scheunert und A. Trautmann, 1987).

Development and functions of muscles

I would now like to explain the development and contraction of muscles in detail for particularly interested readers. The lessons are helpful in order to better understand the rest of the chapter, but they aren't absolutely necessary.

Muscles are first divided up into separate myofibrills, and these in turn into sarcomeres. The smallest functioning units within a sarcomere are actin filaments and myosin filaments. For each contraction of the muscle, actin filaments are pushed into myosin

filaments. When the muscles relax, they slide apart again.

Explanation: The myosin filaments form an energy-supplying complex at corresponding trap centers of the actin filaments in the presence of Ca++. The myosin heads bend down at a 45° angle. Actin filaments und myosin filaments are pushed into each other. Then the myosin heads give off adenosine diphosphate and phosphorus. After this they lack energy and the little myosin heads disengage from the actin filaments and take on adenosine triphosphate (ATP). Afterwards they split into adenosine diphosphate and phosphorus and return to their original configuration. A new muscle cycle can begin.

Experiments have shown that the muscle can develop its greatest strength by means of normal prestretching. The ideal interlocking between the actin and myosin filaments takes place when as many myosin filaments as possible have overlapped the actin filaments and are in contact with them.

Excessive stretching or straining is not beneficial for the development of strength in the muscle. By excessive stretching of the muscle, the optimal interlocking of filaments cannot take place. If the myosin heads don't have contact with the actin filaments, then it is logical that they won't be able to attach to each other. Also with severe shortening of the muscle, i. e. of the length of the sarcomere, effective contraction can no longer take place, since the myosin filaments can not be contracted any further. In addition, straining off the surrounding supply systems also hampers the exchange of ions in the muscle, which leads to increased muscle soreness (Allen 2004)

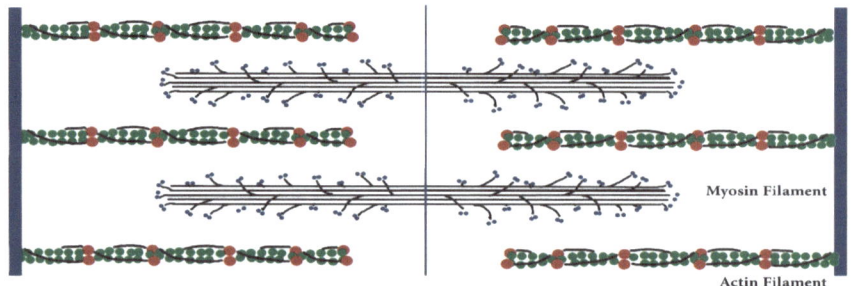

The sarcomere, the smallest functioning unit of a muscle. Actin filaments und myosin filaments slide freely into each other.

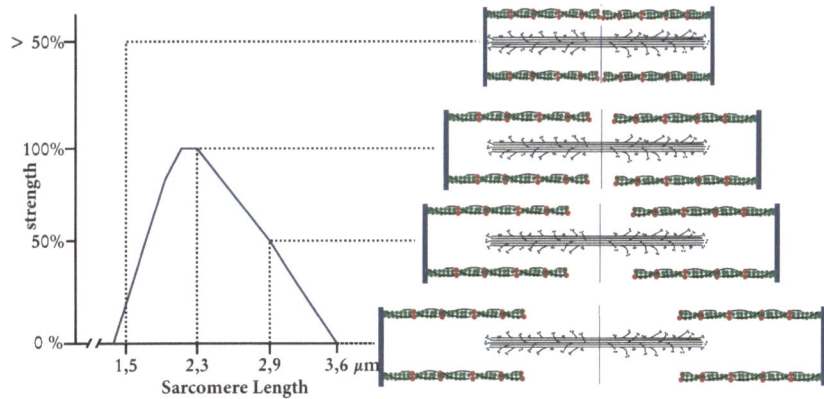

Developing the strength of a muscle depends on the interlocking of actin and myosin filaments. The greatest development of this strength takes place when as many myosin filament heads are connected to actin filaments as possible. (Modified according to A. Scheunert und A. Trautmann, 1987).

Now the explanation for readers who are less medically inclined:

The muscle develops its greatest strength in a normal body position. If single muscles or groups of muscles are severely stretched or pushed together, a powerful contraction is no longer possible. This fact gives us the logical explanation for Brügger's chain, which begins with muscle tension, then muscle inflammation and finally degeneration of the muscles and tendons when the body is forced into a constant, extreme position. For example, the horse's neck muscles with his head pulled toward his chest are overstretched in the topline, while the area under the neck is severely compressed.

A review of the important points:

• Muscle fibers are made up of sarcomeres, which are comprised of actin and myosin filaments.

• When muscles contract, actin and myosin filaments interlock; they glide apart when the muscle relaxes.

• The muscle works effectively with normal stretching, but it works poorly when stretched or strained excessively.

Tips:

• **Try to avoid riding your horse in positions that overstretch certain muscle groups and strain others. A very extreme example of this is rollkur or hyperflexion of the horse's neck. The muscles of the topline are over-stretched, while the area under the neck is severely compressed.**

• **During lessons involving extreme collec-tion, such as piaffe and levade, the horse should be able the carry his nose a hand's width in front of the vertical. It is absolutely necessary during these lessons, which require extraordinary strength, not to**

hinder the muscles from carrying out their function by forced stretching or straining.

Energy conversion in the muscle

Awareness of the different ways the muscle can convert energy into a muscle contraction is important in any discussion about training methods. ATP is the carrier of this energy. The availability of ATP in the muscle is limited, and it is expended when the muscle works, which means that it has to be constantly synthesized. Creatine phosphate is available in high concentrations as a phosphorus reservoir. In order to synthesize ATP, the muscle needs energy, however. This is supplied by glucose (dextrose).

The use or breaking down of glucose is effected by various mechanisms:

• On the one hand, there is the aerobic energy conversion. This means that in the presence of oxygen, glucose is split into CO_2 und H_2O. This split is very effective. It supplies 38 mole of ATP per mole of glucose. In addition, the degrada-tion products CO_2 and H_2O can easily be transported by the cardiocascular system and breathed out through the lungs.

• On the other hand, glucose cannot be used without the presence of oxygen. This anaerobic conversion is not very effective. Per mole of glucose, the muscle only gets 2 mole of ATP. Lactic acid is the degradation product, which is difficult to dispose of in the body.

Finally, a part of the muscle energy can still be derived from the aerobic breakdown of fatty acids. Particularly slow twitch muscle fibers that are less fatigable, as well as only partially fast twitch muscle fibers that are also not fatigable, use fatty acids as their energy supplier.

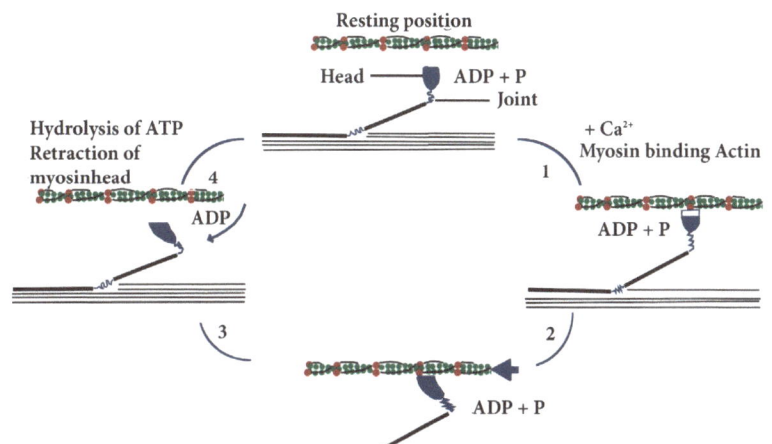

Binding the myosin head to the actin filament

If the aerobic energy conversion offers such clear advantages, why does the body have to fall back on other ways to convert energy at all? Unfortunately, the aerobic energy system is simply too slow. It takes approximately 2 – 3 minutes for the increased oxygen transfer to reach the muscle when muscle activity rises. Until that time, the muscle metabolism has to be covered anaerobically. At the beginning of every increasing muscle activity, the body has to sustain a lack of oxygen for this short period. Duing this time essential ions are consumed and lactic acid is produced. If the muscle activity remains at the same level, then after 2 – 3 minutes the energy conversion can continue aerobically. A steady state results between the time when ATP splits and when it forms. Working muscles can be maintained in this balance for a long time. The reservoirs of ions can be refilled and the body disposes of the resulting lactic acid, both while the muscles are still working and afterwards.

Almost everyone who swims or jogs has experienced the feeling during the first 2 – 3 minutes of activity that the task is just too daunting. Involuntarily, you think that you're just too tired to do anything athletic on that day. But if you continue to exercise with the initial intensity, you will see in the next few minutes that the aerobic/anaerobic steady state kicks in. Suddenly the sport seems easy and for a while, until exhaustion sets in, you can swim or jog with pleasure. If you increase the exertion continuously, however, without a steady state being able to establish itself, soon you will feel that you're going to drown or you'll have to give up.

If muscle activity constantly increases, whether fast or slow, or if lasting, hard work is being done and it is not possible for an aerobic-anaerobic steady state to develop, oxygen and ions, which are absolutely necessary for muscle function, cannot be made available quickly enough. The muscle is over acidified, because too much lactic acid has been produced. Horses that have reached a state of complete exhaustion show a blood lactate concentration of 20 -25 mole/l, compared to the levels in a relaxed state of about 1 mole/l in the venous blood. The amount of lactic acid present when the aerobic-anaerobic threshold is reached amounts to about .4m-mole/ l (Frey und Hildenbrand, 1994 / Marées, 1981 / Heipertz-Hengst, 1999). A severe calcium deficiency also develops when the muscles are overstrained (Allen 2004).

The effect lactate has on muscle oxygenation is described by Markworth (1992):

"The price ... is the high blood lactate concentration in the muscle cells. Since lactic acid is a weak acid, the cell milieu becomes sour. This, in turn, causes the highly sensitive enzyme glycolysis to stop its activity when a certain level of acidity in the cell has been reached. Without this enzyme, absolutely no ATP can be resynthesized. The muscle cell ceases all activity, causing the subjective signs of exhaustion."

For a long time, people thought that sore muscles were an indication of the presence of a high blood lactate concentration. This opinion seems to be outdated, because signs of muscle soreness have been found in muscles that are not hyperacidic. In addition, sore muscles don't occur until 12 to 24 hours after an activity, when most of the lactate has already disappeared. High amounts of lactic acid have been measured without sore muscles, after 400 m races for example, as well as sore muscles without an increase of lactic acid, like mountain races, for example (Marées, 1994). Therefore, the cause of sore muscles must have more to do with the type of movement or activity. Today it is assumed that the major cause of sore muscles has to be a lack of intramuscular coordination. Especially unaccustomed braking movements trigger severe muscle soreness.

Have you ever been mountain climbing? Then you must have noticed that the most intense muscle soreness was not caused by the muscles you used to climb up the mountain, but rather the muscles you had to use to brake yourself going back down. Climbing down a mountain frequently elicits the feeling that your muscles are not quite under control, even though you don't feel all that exhausted.

Lunges are another good example. If you haven't practiced lunges, you are usually astonished that it only takes a few to cause extremely painful muscle soreness the next day.

Due to the unaccustomed shearing of the muscle fibers, which happens when the muscles are strained, the sarcomeres are burdened excessively, even damaged, causing tiny micro-ruptures in the muscle (Markworth, 1992 / Marées, 1994 / Müller-Wohlfahrt, 1996). In addition, the shearing of the sarcomeres causes an interruption in the exchange of ions, especially of calcium and phosphate, in turn causing the tiniest muscle unit to die (Allen 2004). This damage to the muscle fibers brings about inflamation locally and finally to edemas. Sore muscles are caused primarily by the micro-ruptures themselves, and secondarily by the swelling and edemas, which put pressure on the nerve cells (Proske and Morgan 2001). It is still unclear whether these micro-ruptures heal with or without scarring. In fact, each scar would lessen the elasticity of the muscle. If this is the case, every time sore muscles result from some activity, it will mean permanent damage to the muscular system. (Springorum, 1986).

Similarly, Müller-Wohlfart und Kübler (1996) wrote:

"Especially in professional soccer, people thought for a long time that properly sore muscles were proof of good, intensive training. Today we know that is completely wrong. We have established that sore muscles are a sign of minor tissue damage, which causes the discomfort, and not "just" an accumulation of blood lactate and metabolic slags. This puts the muscle into a condition in which it increasingly loses the ability to stretch and contract. You can recognize a good soccer trainer by the way he increases his players' training exercises and then stops just before they get sore muscles."

Considering the fact that it still isn't completely clear exactly what triggers sore muscles, this sounds more like wishful thinking, of course. Sore muscles cannot always be avoided in training. Certainly a reasonable training plan can help avoid sudden over-stressing. During daily training, the rider has to have an instinctive feel for the horse. He or she is in the best position to notice when the horse isn't able to perform the required movements as easily as at the beginning of the training session. When in doubt, remember the slogan: "Less is more". Then you can be sure you aren't inflicting any damage, and you can continue the training where you left off the next day.

Unfortunately, there are still many riders who make hardly any demands on their horses throughout the week. Then once or twice on the weekend they appear and ride the poor creature ragged. These riders should spare their four-legged partners this kind of torture, because, besides severe exhaustion and the accumulation of lactic acid in the muscles and rupturing the muscle fibers, they are accomplishing nothing. Instead of some kind of ill-conceived conditioning, the horse suffers lasting damage from this training strategy.

Judicious, systematic training increases the effectiveness of the aerobic energy conversion system step by step. Along with an improved supply of nutrients to the muscles, the sarcomeres start to multiply within a week as well. With an increased number of sarcomeres, the muscles are able to counteract the shearing of the muscle fibers. This is how the muscle work required for braking movements can be trained. At the end of a hiking vacation, you won't get sore muscles any more from climbing down the mountain. Even the number of lunges you can do without suffering from muscle soreness will increase the more often you do them.

A review of the important points:

- Muscle metabolism occurs aerobically with oxygen and anaerobically without oxygen.

- Aerobic metabolism is more effective, but slower.

- The amount produced from aerobic metabolism can be trained.

- Muscle soreness is caused by a lack of muscle coordination and eccentric positions that the body is not accustomed to.

- Unaccustomed shearing of the muscle fibers leads to a poor supply of ions and finally to micro-ruptures in the muscle fibers.

- Through training, the sarcomeres multiply and are then able to counteract severe shearing of the muscles.

Tips:

- Repeat training stimuli twice a week rather than training to the point of exhaustion.

- For an improved supply of nutrients to the muscles, you need a continuous increase in the training demands.

- The proliferaton of sarcomeres will remain for a long time. This is why intramuscular coordination can be maintained even during breaks in training. You will see that your horse, even after longer periods of rest, will keep the same level of balance and collection. He might be out of breath more quickly, however.

Three types of twitch muscle fibers

The skeletal muscles of the mammal consist of three different types of twitch muscle fibers.

- Fast, fatigable but strong, thick twitch muscle fibers with a lot of mostly anaerobic energy consumption.

- Fast, less fatigable, thin twitch muscle fibers with high, partially aerobic but also anaerobic energy consumption.

- Slow, thin twitch muscle fibers resistant to fatigue with negligible aerobic energy consumption.

Musculature that develops a lot of strength also uses a lot of energy, which can hardly be covered aerobically, whereas thin endurance musculature works much more efficiently. These endurance muscles can get by with oxygen for energy production and are resistant to fatigue. Systematic training can influence which types of twitch muscle fibers are trained more.

In most riding disciplines the problem arises that to varying degrees two types of musculature are needed: one for strength and one for endurance. If the muscles needed for strength are trained too much, the horse's endurance is adversely affected, because strength musculature uses too much energy. For this reason, long-distance riders rarely engage in strength training with their horses. Their horses are endowed primarily with long, thin muscles that are resistant to fatigue. Thick muscles for strength would use up precious energy. The event rider must try to find the golden mean between both extremes. His horse also needs endurance for cross-country and long stretches of galloping. However, for jumping and dressage, the horse cannot perform without muscles for strength.

Now the dressage horse needs considerably more strength, yet many sequences of movements require endurance and agility as well. However, because of its high use of energy, strength training requires special instinctive feel from the rider. The only way to train a dressage horse successfully so that he can master most of the lessons in the aerobic zone is through many years of consistent muscle building and training of his muscular coordination.

At first, through systematic strength training, a clear increase of the horse's strength can be ascertained, without a thickening of the twitch muscle fibers. The explanation for this is the improvement of intramuscular coordination - the result of the training. Later, the twitch muscle fibers do increase in thickness, which causes the imposing appearance of a well-trained dressage horse.

A review of the important points:

• There are different types of twitch muscle fibers for the corresponding requirements of different equestrian disciplines.

• Dressage horses need an increase of strong, thick twitch muscle fibers, which are more quickly fatigued.

• Training improves the intramuscular coordination first, then the thickness of the muscles is improved.

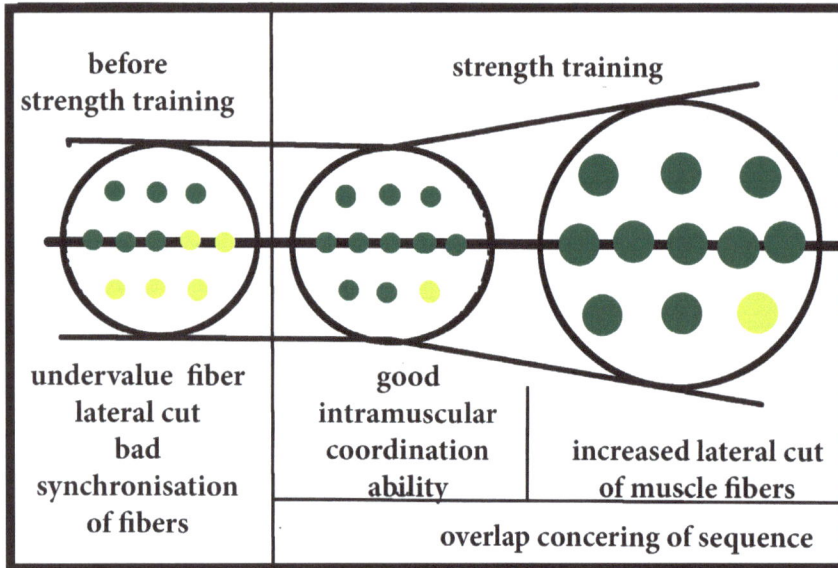

before strength training	strength training	
undervalue fiber lateral cut bad synchronisation of fibers	good intramuscular coordination ability	increased lateral cut of muscle fibers
	overlap concering of sequence	

The effects of strength training: When the muscles are untrained, they don't contract all of the muscle fibers simultaneously. As the training continues, the synchronization of the muscle fibers improves, and it isn't until much later that a clear increase of the sarcomeres can be measured in the cross-section of the muscle fiber (according to G. Frey and E. Hildenbrandt, 1994).

Tips:

• **Horses that are trained for a particular riding discipline will have a different appearance. Whereas a dressage horse has primarily round, thick, powerful muscles, horses trained for endurance sports will have long, thin muscles.**

Further references:

Allen, D.G. 'Skeletal muscle function: role of ionic changes in fatigue, damage and disease', Clin Exp Pharmacol Physiol, 31 (8) (2004), 485-93.

Boening, D. 'Muskelkater', Med Monatsschr Pharm, 26 (5) (2003), 167-71.

Proske, U. and Morgan, D.L. 'Muscle damage from eccentric exercise: mechanism, mechanical signs, adaptation and clinical applications', J Phusiol., 537 (Pt. 2) (2001), 333-45.

Scheunert, A. and Trautmann, A. Lehrbuch der Vetrinaer-Physiologie. (Berlin: Paul Parey Verlag, 1987).

Muscles

Tendons, Ligaments and Joints

The muscles are not the only organs in the body that can be stabilized, strengthened and enlarged in circumference. The same effect can be had on tendons, ligaments and joints (Ivers 1983). As described in the previous chapter, dressage, besides being an end in itself, gives the horse the means to carry his rider more easily and balance him effortlessly. However, the horse is not able to do this from one day to the next. In the beginning, the sequence of movements in dressage requires a great deal of strength, putting the muscles, tendons and joints under stress in ways that the horse hadn't used them before.

Therefore it is absolutely necessary to think about how to teach the horse the movements in dressage in small doses and with great care. If you take the time and effort to include the tendons, ligaments and joints in a reasonable training program, you will soon notice that they are getting stronger. Otherwise there is a danger of damaging these structures by suddenly overburdening them.

In this context there are frequent complaints about problems that dressage horses have with their tendons, ligaments and joints. Here are a few examples:

Arthritis in the hock (bone spavin)
Caused by overburdening the hock during collection without using the correct bend of the haunches. If the horse doesn't have enough strength to maintain collection and with it the bend of the haunches for the time that the rider requires, the horse substitutes the bend of the hip and knee joints by bending the hock. Over time the hock is damaged by the poor physiological (protective) position that the horse is forced to take.

Inflammation of the tendon's sheath and thoroughpins
Tendon sheaths, which are severely stressed by excessive movement of the joints, are easily overburdened. The result is inflammation in the spaces that are filled with fluid. Watery synovial fluid (joint fluid and fluid from the tendon sheath) builds up. Ultimately there is a painful swelling of the joint caused by the inflammation of different tendon sheaths (called windgalls or thoroughpins).

Stretched ligaments and arthritis
Lateral movements like shoulder-in, half-passes, pirouettes, etc., require the legs to take on more weight in a tilted position, and this often in a faster gait. The severe, lateral burden on the tendons, ligaments and joints, as well as the tilted movement that follows, must also be trained very slowly. Otherwise, stretched ligaments and arthritis are the immediate result.

Sprains
The condition of the footing of some arenas at horse shows often leaves a lot to be desired, or at least it is not what the horse is accustomed to at home. It makes sense to include cross-country rides on different types of terrain at home in your training schedule. Not only will the health of the horse benefit from this, but your results at shows will be better, because the horse will have learned after a while how to present itself properly on any type of surface.

Rupture of tendon fibers
This occurs when the musculature is too weak and the tendons too thin to stabilize the legs. In cases like this either the muscles are generally too untrained, or, more frequently, it comes from fatigue. With a fresh horse, the musculature has a certain basic tension that ensures that muscles and tendons cannot be stretched too far. But if the musculature is fatigued, the muscles and the tendons can be stretched without control and then possibly over-stretched. Sooner or later there is no more elasticity and individual tendon fibers rupture. In extreme cases, the entire tendon might rupture.

Unfortunately, damage to joints and ligaments can be persistent to irreparable. Ligaments that have been overstretched are usually sensitive and unstable afterwards. They can only be marginally stabilized with a huge amount of time and effort in training.

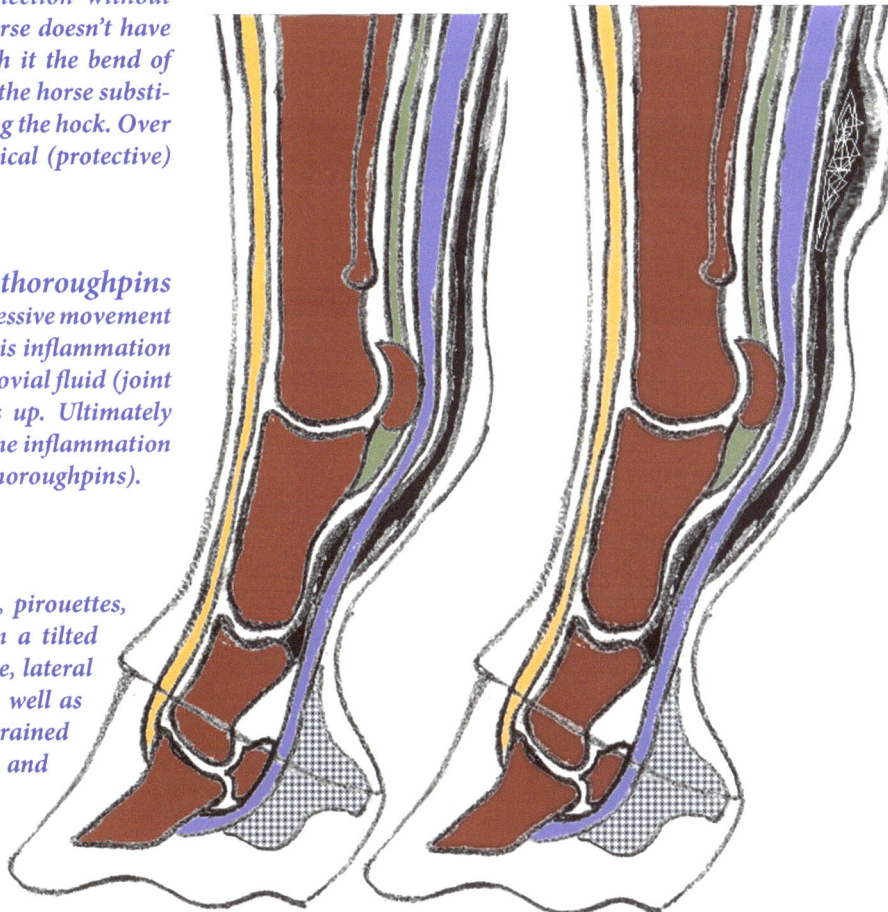

The effect that too much stress on the joints has is inflammation, which causes, first of all, an increase in the amount of fluid in the joints. At this point the inflammation is visible in the thoroughpins (windgalls) in the hock, and can be medically treated and possibly cured with slow conditioning exercises (Stashak, 1989). If this phase is ignored, however, damage to the joint cartilage will appear soon. Joint cartilage cannot be regenerated, so in place of the old cartilage, a kind of substitute tissue starts to grow. This tissue will never be as resilient as the original cartilage.

Tendon damage is another issue, however. With enough patience, tendons can be made completely resilient again. However, this is a very long process. With less than a year of rest and slow conditioning, there have been very few horses up to now that have been able to return to high performance sports. Optically the tendon appears to be healed early on. There is a great temptation to put too much stress on the tendon too early. Still, the chaotically structured scar tissue simply needs time to shape itself in the direction of the fibers. Until then, the former elasticity simply is not there (Steiner, 1982).

A review of the important points:

- By attempting to train too quickly or without the proper knowledge, damage can be quickly done to the tendons, ligaments and joints.

- Damage to the joints and ligaments is usually irreparable.

- Damage to the tendons can often be completely healed with enough patience.

Tips for training tendons, ligaments and joints:

- In addition to normal sessions of dressage training, trail riding is excellent exercise for the tendons, ligaments and joints. Various conditions underfoot and the incline of the terrain offer plenty of stimuli for the biomechanical system of the horse. If you choose an easy gait (walk, trot or even a calm, controlled canter), then the danger of overstraining is minimal.

- Even the pasture offers many training effects for the biomechanical system. Along with the relief they give to the body, both the pasture and the trails are balm for the athlete's soul. In the meantime, the old myth about not being able to use a dressage horse for sports if he is allowed out in the pasture regularly has been refuted by a myriad of successful athletes.

- Training in an equine swimming pool is no longer recommended for tendons and joints at the moment. Despite the positive effect that swimming clearly has on the cardiovascular system, it is relatively useless for the tendons and ligaments due to the lack of resistance in the water. This training and rehabilitation method should rather be used in combination with conventional training, because an otherwise well-trained athlete would climb out of the swimming pool with weak tendons and ligaments. Of what use is a horse in excellent condition if his legs don't measure up to the performance requirements? However, spraying the horse's legs down with cold water or letting him walk in shallow water after a workout are very good practices. Cold water stimulates the circulation and promotes the regeneration of stressed structures. Additionally, the resistance of the water is a good stimulus for the musculature required for strength.

Further reference:

Stashak, T.S. Adams' Lahmheit bei Pferden. H. Wissdorf (Hannover: Schaper Verlag, 1989).

Motivating the dressage horse

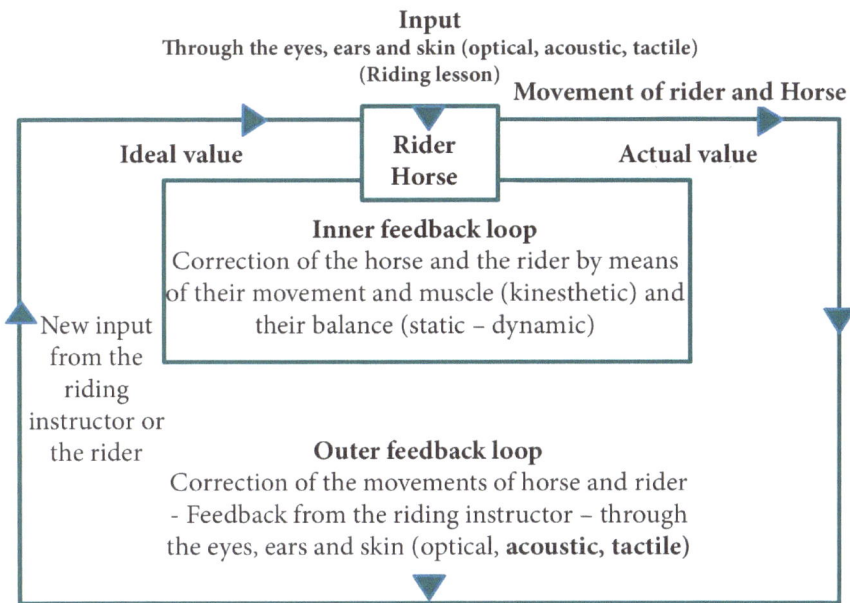

Input
Through the eyes, ears and skin (optical, acoustic, tactile)
(Riding lesson)

Movement of rider and Horse

Ideal value | Rider Horse | **Actual value**

Inner feedback loop
Correction of the horse and the rider by means of their movement and muscle (kinesthetic) and their balance (static – dynamic)

New input from the riding instructor or the rider

Outer feedback loop
Correction of the movements of horse and rider
- Feedback from the riding instructor – through the eyes, ears and skin (optical, **acoustic, tactile**)

Learning according to the closed loop model
The horse and rider are carrying out a certain sequence of movements. They are correcting themselves (they are running through an inner closed loop); On the other hand, the riding instructor gives suggestions for improvement (this is the outer closed loop). After the correction, the sequence of movements improves. The closed loop starts all over again (modified according to E. Meyners, 1982).

Motivation is an important factor in accomplishing performance goals. Not only does the rider have to be motivated, but also the horse. Many horses are naturally endowed with a general enthusiasm about working and learning. Others have to be cajoled into cooperating with the rider. For a high-performance athlete in dressage, of course it is an advantage for him to belong to the former category. Such horses, who literally offer themselves to their riders, are not necessarily easier to train. The real challenge for the rider is not to overwhelm them, while at the same time maintaining their high motivation. Otherwise these eager horses are already past their best performance potential before they've reached the prime age for a dressage horse, which is about 12 years, according to Rainer Klimke (1969). Yet even for the lazier horse, there are ways to get him to like dressage.

For all horses it is important to learn a certain automatism of movement. Specialists also call this "learning according to the closed loop model".

In the beginning, the horse and rider are quite uncertain. They have to concentrate fully on every detail of the lesson. Influences from the outside that get through to the horse and rider disrupt their concentration and lead to mistakes. It follows that at this stage, a correct execution of the lessons is only possible under optimal conditions.

Every time the closed loop repeats itself, the sequence of movements becomes more secure and self-confident. Piece by piece the movements move into the subconscious part of the brain. In the end, the horse and rider are able to execute the sequence of movements successfully even under changed or poor conditions.

The good news about the closed loop model goes something like this: "Practice makes perfect". It is very important for dressage horses to learn the automatism of movements. At horse shows you have to be prepared for changing, even difficult circumstances. If the horse has practiced the sequence of movements so well that they are playing through in his subconscious, then the noise, crowds, music, different footing, etc., will not lead to mistakes as often while he is performing. The automatism of movements gives nervous, overeager horses security, and lazy horses are motivated to cooperate.

Trail riding serves as mental training and for relaxation of the horse

Jumping as both mental and strength training

Mental training of the horse

The mental training of the horse, and especially the young horse, should definitely be included in the annual planning, because it takes up a lot of time. To prepare a horse for a show, it's not enough to train him in his familiar surroundings at home. Horses must also see and experience changing conditions. In order to do this, it is crucial to grasp every opportunity to ride in different places. Simply training at home in different rings or arenas is not enough. If you don't just want to write off the first horse shows as events for learning or acclimatization, it makes sense to take the time to trailer the horse to unfamiliar equine facilities. Workshops at one of these facilities would be a great opportunity not only for learning, but also for getting used to "new" terrain for several days. This would increase the training stimuli and acclimatization effect.

In addition, dressage horses are also grateful for a change in their daily work. Occasional jumping, regular trail rides and once in a while training on the racetrack, even at a higher speed, develop the horse physically and mentally. Trail rides and especially galloping at a high speed should be a regular part of the training schedule. Nervous horses get adrenalized in the beginning. When they get used to this kind of exercise, it does an excellent job relaxing them. The next day the horses are usually contented, relaxed and able to unwind. (Springorum, 1986).

In the context of motivation and mental training, the dressage horse's "leisure time" should be taken into consideration. The rule of thumb: The more in tune it is with the horse's true nature, the better. As often and as long as possible, horses should have the chance to recover out-of-doors grazing in a pasture. To stand in a stall 23 hours a day, and then to be ridden one hour a day in the higher gaits

is completely against the physiology of the horse. In nature, horses move the entire day, mostly at a walk. Treat your horse to regular pasture time every day, in groups or at least in pairs! Your reward will be not only better physical health for your equine partner, since all structures of the biomechanical system are more evenly supplied with blood, but his mental fitness will also improve. In the most natural surroundings possible, opportunities abound that will strengthen the horse's skills and character. (Schönfelder, 1982).

Mental blocks of fear

In order to get a horse used to changing conditions, training must take place in small steps. Whether it is weather, noise, different footing or going out to pasture, etc., when the opportunity presents itself, you should expose your horse to these stimuli slowly and in small doses. Otherwise he might simply be overwhelmed, and instead of reacting with self-confidence, he will react with fear. Take the time to desensitize your horse by leading him over tarps, plastic baby pools, water, logs and show him for example plastic bags, umbrellas, balloons.

Fear is every bit as negative an experience for horses as it is for people. Not only does it lead to mental knee-jerk reactions, it also blocks the whole body. Along with a strong feeling of reluctance and refusal, there is a clear, measurable rise in the horse's pulse rate, changes in the skin temperature, blood pressure, respiration, muscle tension and a decrease in his ability to deal with his surroundings (Meyners, 1982). The horse is not being stubborn when he can't perform in fearful situations; he is simply unable to react any other way.

**Maintaining horses in small groups keeps them healthy
and more willing to perform for their riders.**

Fear is one of a number of reasons for poor behavior in horses. Other reasons might also be pain, excessive demands, boredom, etc. (Schönfelder, 1982). In our many years of riding experience, we have frequently come across unreliable, fearful and unmotivated horses that are suffering from painful illnesses. Often these horses spend years in training with very unsatisfactory results until their illness is discovered. Spinal diseases, arthritis of the joints, illnesses of the respiratory system, many metabolic diseases and a lot more can insidiously set in and go undetected for years. These diseases are even difficult for the veterinarian to diagnose in the beginning, because there is no clear tissue damage. But the rider can feel that there is something wrong. The sensitive feel and intuition of the rider and trainer are the best barometers for motivation. Any concerns the rider might have, even vague ones, should be seriously investigated. The most satisfying feeling for a rider is when both partners are happy and in the best of health.

A review of the important points:

- Learning automatism of movement increases motivation. It makes skittish horses more self-confident, and lazy horses work harder.

- The mental training of a show horse should include visits to unfamiliar riding facilities.

- Even a horse needs "leisure time". If you plan this free time properly, you will find it becomes a useful part of the horse's training.

- Horses that are overwhelmed frequently become fearful, and are not only stubborn, but also downright blocked.

Tips:

- **Practice makes perfect! Repeat lessons regularly. Every repetition improves the horse's coordination and mental confidence.**

- **Early on in your horse's training you should transport him to unfamiliar training facilities so that he can become accustomed to changes and not feel threatened by them.**

- **Insert alternative training methods, such as jumping, trail riding and possibly even the racetrack, into your training program. This boosts your horse's motivation very positively and is excellent conditioning for him.**

- **Treat your horse's fears seriously. Slow down the pace of his training and go back to an exercise where he still felt confident. Start over from there. If you can't get rid of the fear blocking his performance, you won't be able to progress with training.**

- **If your horse continues to be skittish, call on the experts to examine him for possible health issues.**

Desensitization practice

Training

General basics for training

In principle, training can be regarded as the act of pushing the body out of homeostasis. Homeostasis is the state of equilibrium between what the body is capable of and what the environment demands of it. After displacement, a new adjustment preferably to a higher level of strength, endurance or skill should be attained. A one-time workout of the body with the corresponding fatigue is followed by a recovery phase, a positive adjustment phase to a higher level of performance, and finally a negative adjustment phase back to the original level of performance, as shown in Figure 8.

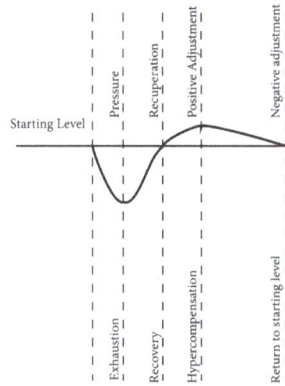

Figure 8
Displacement of the organism out of homeostasis due to training stimuli (according to G. Frey and E. Hildenbrandt, 1994)

If you want your horse's performance to improve, the next training session should take place before the phase of negative adjustment sets in. For example, it is not enough to go out and climb a hill with your horse every two weeks, because by the time you go climbing again, the horse's condition has shrunk back to what it was before. On the other hand, having the horse climb the same hill every 4 – 5 days also doesn't provide enough progressive improvement in his condition. Over the long term the organism gets accustomed to the workout. For real growth and improvement in performance, the training stimuli have to be a lot more. You should either climb the hill more often, or find a longer trail up the hill.

The deciding factor for training success, in addition to the quality, is also the quantity of the training, in other words the frequency. It has been shown that the organism adjusts better to frequent training sessions with small workouts than to infrequent training with a substantial workout.

It is more expedient to include new movements in your dressage training session every other day for a few minutes, rather than practice them once a week for an entire hour. In the meantime, when training jumpers, the practice of clearing many small jumps on several days of the week has become well established, as opposed to "going for broke" once a week over the highest obstacles.

A review of the important points:
- Part of training is pushing the body beyond its current level of performance.
- An increase in the performance level can only be attained by constantly increasing the training requirements.
- The quality and quantity of training must be taken into consideration in the training plan.

Tips:

- **Train regularly, but in intervals.**

- **Increase the performance requirements of your horse slowly and continuously.**

- **Start with simple lessons and increase the level of difficulty bit by bit.**

Taking a rewarding rest break

The most controversial point concerning horses' training is the rest period between the individual training units. It makes sense that training stimuli won't have the desired effect if the rest intervals are so long that the organism falls back to its original performance level every time. See figure 9:

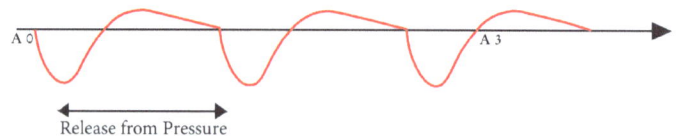

Figure 9

It is just as bad if the rest intervals are too short. The horse barely has the chance to recover from one training unit to the next, and the organism doesn't have enough time to adapt to a higher performance level. See Figure 10:

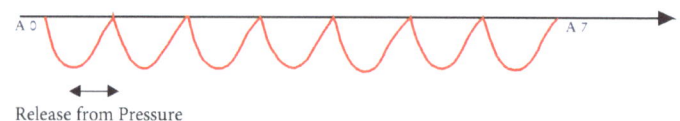

Figure 10

If you choose to have very short intervals between workouts, or don't allow any time for rest, then your training will have an adverse effect on your horse and his condition will start to deteriorate. If a horse does moderate dressage exercises every day until the point of exhaustion, his organism won't have the opportunity to regenerate and starts to decline as a result. This phenomenon is called "over-training". See figure 11:

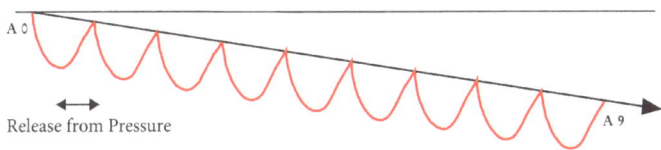

Release from Pressure

Figure 11

In addition to this, when training horses you must constantly take into account the fact that an exhausted horse can't recover to the extent that a human being can. If the horse's biomechanical system is not allowed to recover, the chain of degeneration described by Brügger (see page 8) will set in. Since the horse has to continue to move on all four feet, and even in a state of exhaustion has to be prepared to flee, damage to muscles, tendons and joints occurs very quickly (Ivers, 1983).

Especially in the show season, many riders tend to switch to a concentrated training plan. A horse show in and of itself represents a stressful situation, and if the rider wants to correct the mistakes from the last show the following week, time-outs for rest and recuperation will frequently be neglected. When in doubt, it is always better to cancel an unimportant show than to risk your horse's health. In this way there is more time to correct mistakes.

Ideally, an increase in performance skills occurs when the new training stimuli are used at the peak of the horse's positive adjustment to the new level of performance. See figure 12:

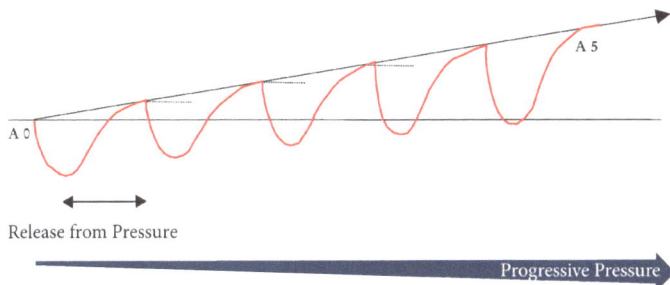

Release from Pressure

Progressive Pressure

Figure 12

Training with rest intervals

What is the ideal length of time for training intervals? In track and field athletics, the normal interval is 48 hours for training that takes place 3 – 4 times a week. Frey und Hildenbrand (1994) give a few factors that influence the distance between rest intervals:

- **Physical predisposition and condition**
- **Type of workout (cardiovascular system, musculature and nervous system)**
- **Intensity, length of time and comprehensiveness of the workout**
- **Frequency of the training (recovery after the previous workout)**
- **Living conditions (sleep, nourishment, etc.)**

Once again, clearly, the ideal barometer for this is still the intuitive feel of the rider. The more routined the rider is and the more frequently he practices with his horse, whether it is dressage training or balancing training activities, the more quickly he will have a certain feeling for the resilience of the horse.

Despite the most modern training methods, it is advisable to make the overall training program flexible. Even in track and field athletics it has been shown that short-term training is not as long lasting as training that has been built up over a long period of time. The principles of longevity and regularity should always be the highest goals for training. Short-term growth of strength and endurance are easier to attain, yet tendons, ligaments and joints require a much longer time to adjust to the new demands.

For example, a young horse might be able to show collection very quickly by means of systematic strength training. However, he won't be able to show this collection for very long if the joints and, more specifically, the hocks are not resilient enough for the stress and are damaged permanently.

In order to weigh rewarding rest periods against expedient training stimuli, the rider and trainer need an instinctive feel for the horse. It is common knowledge that very long rest intervals for recuperation have a negative effect on the horse's condition. It used to be common to give horses a "vacation" of several weeks in winter. Surely this also had something to do with the fact that many riders didn't have access to an indoor riding arena for training. Yet to take the horse completely out of his training rhythm for such a long time has proven to be less than helpful. Besides losing his speed, strength and stamina, he also loses coordinated muscle movement (Springorum, 1986). Rebuilding all of these qualities doesn't only take a lot of time; the whole organism pays a price, not to mention the danger of injury to a horse that has lost his condition. Therefore it makes more sense to maintain a smaller workload. Regular, relaxing work and quiet trail rides help the horse to start off the next show season with a tranquil and stress-free attitude.

A review of the important points:

- Rest breaks are an important part of training.
- Rest intervals that are too long have a negative effect on the horse's general condition.
- Rest intervals that are too short lead to physical exhaustion and poor performance.
- Training intervals must be adjusted individually. One rule of thumb: every 3rd days a new training stimulus should be introduced.

Tips:

- Allow your horse to take regular rest breaks. These can be adjusted individually.

- For breaks in training, anything is permitted that provides relaxation and pleasure for the horse. They recover well in a pasture, trail riding, free jumping or doing other diverse training activities.

Figure 13
Training aid trail riding 1
Musculature for impulsion is trained by uphill work. In addition, stretching the topline has gymnastic value for the horse.

Figure 14
Training aid trail riding 2
Downhill work uses the musculature of the hindquarters in a way similar to collected exercises.

Training aids

Of course it is just as important to think about the quality of the training. A dressage horse learns about dressage by practicing it, and, first and foremost, a jumper should jump. Thoroughbred stud farms place great value on having extensive pastures where the foals and yearlings have ample opportunities to gallop. However, balancing training activities such as jumping and trail riding can assist individual training elements. If trail riding, jumping and galloping, etc., are included wisely in the training plan, they are extremely beneficial for dressage work. In addition, the whole organism including the mental abilities of the horse is challenged. Trail riding serves, on the one hand, to relax the horse. On the other hand, trail riding assists training for strength and endurance if stretches of hill climbing are systematically built into it.

Now let's think about training aids for dressage work. The most important training aid is the dressage work itself. Two to four times a week a horse should be worked moderately with dressage exercises, depending on his temperament and condition. The greatest effects of training are achieved when you set a very specific goal for a few weeks and then, building on that, expand the workload later.

Training objective: Impulsion

For example, you could make working on impulsion your initial training goal. It would make sense to put work on collection on hold, and in the next few weeks focus primarily on "forward riding".

Even on trail rides you can practice your training goal "impulsion". On level stretches with good footing, many horses are much more willing to go forwards with impulsion than in the riding hall. And of course there is more straightaway for a longer distance when you are riding cross-country. It is much more effective for the development of impulsion to be able to urge the horse with both legs into both reins for a longer period of time. Besides, the one-sided pressure from the inner leg while doing turns in the riding hall is no longer there. On the trail the horse also learns how to maintain his impulsion while cantering over uneven ground.

Of course for the development of impulsion, the racetrack is ideal, not only for galloping but also for trotting work.

Even jumping can be good training for the energetic strides of the hind legs. Once or twice a week doing a gymnastic workout over small jumps proves to be beneficial for the dressage horse. This kind of work stimulates the horse's suppleness and the static as well as the dynamic strength of the hindquarters.

For many horses, free-jumping is more fun than jumping with a rider. However, there are horses that "freak out" while free-jumping, so for them, jumping under the control of a rider makes more sense.

Finally, the greater resistance in water makes a good training exercise for the driving and carrying power of the hind legs. It is enough to have the horse walking in shallow water. As a welcome addition to strength training, cold water stimulates the circulatory system in the legs.

A review of the important points:
- The main method to train dressage is by practicing dressage.
- However, dressage training is more effective if alternative training methods are used such as jumping, trail riding or water training.

Tips:

- **Work on specific dressage lessons and repeat them regularly.**

- **Be sensitive to your horse's needs and try out things that she enjoys. Nearly all training methods offer good opportunities to develop the skills necessary to perform dressage movements.**

- **If your horse likes to go trail riding, then train her there. There are a few successful dressage riders who don't have a riding hall available.**

- **Good nerves and sure-footedness are just as important to a dressage horse as the correct performance of the dressage movements themselves.**

Further references:

Götz C. 2008. Praxishandbuch Freispringen Gymnastik, Training, Abwechslung, Cadmos Verlag Brunsbeck

Ettl R. 2008. Horse-Agility - Spielerisch und anspruchsvoll trainieren. Müller-Rüschlikon, Stuttgart

Strength training

Compared to horses that are ridden in endurance sports like long-distance riding and three-day eventing, the dressage horse needs a lot of strength. In equine sports the categories are as follows:

Maximum strength

- The greatest strength that the horse's organism can develop against a type of resistance. For example: The horse's strength when he holds himself in the levade as long as possible. The resistance in this case is gravity.

Explosive power

- The ability of the biomechanical system to overcome resistance with the highest possible speed of contraction. This strength plays a greater role in jumping, although an elevated piaffe and passage require explosive power as well.

Endurance strength

- The ability to complete exercises requiring long-lasting exertion while showing little or no fatigue. For example: Collected exercises that should be done for a longer period of time, such as the combination: collected trot - piaffe – passage – collected trot.

Reactive strength

- This designates the muscle activity that results when, out of a braking, yielding movement, great strength is developed as fast as possible. For example: Passage is the movement that requires the most reactive strength. It is characterized by a fluent change between impulsion and static collection.

Training for maximum strength

Very few riders use their horses for driving nowadays. Horses in front of a wagon that have to pull heavy loads are comparable to track and field athletes doing weight training. This is the only way to make a comparison between the cross training and bodybuilding of human athletes to horse athletes in equestrian sports. The basis of this training is to build the muscle's potential strength to its maximum limit. However, since driving is too time-consuming to use only for the purpose of strength training, and should be learned properly as well, we have to resort to other methods.

Training intramuscular coordination, a prerequisite for training for maximum strength, is significantly more effective for dressage horses. In principle, you could practice with the various collected exercises, since they require the greatest amount of strength. In order to school intramuscular coordination, it's enough to practice.

Figure 15
Training aid jumping 1
During downhill jumping there is a clear bend of the haunches. The maximum strength trained here is good for collected movements in dressage.

Figure 16
Training aid jumping 2
The take-off phase trains not only for explosive power but also for the powerful strides of the hind legs to improve impulsion.

Training for explosive power

Explosive power can best be improved by jumping. Small jumps can often be included in the normal training plan to promote the energetic strides of the hind legs.

Training for stamina and endurance strength

Endurance strength and stamina are what are required most from dressage horses. Either you train them with endurance methods or with interval work.

- Stamina demands a long-lasting workout from the horse. For example, you ride at a collected trot every second or third day for a few minutes. You start with 5 minutes and expand step by step up to 15 minutes at a stretch.

- Another possibility is interval training, which means planning rest intervals between the individual training exercises. Let's take the example of collected trot. With interval training you could start with three sessions of two to three minutes of collected trot. Between the trot repetitions the rider allows his horse to go at a walk for a few minutes. The horse shouldn't completely recover from the exercise; otherwise the next interval won't offer any training stimulus. Later the intervals could be extended to three sessions of four minutes of collected trot, then three sessions of five minutes, etc.

For training endurance strength, climbing hills outside is a very useful exercise. This can be included in endurance training by having the horse gradually climb higher hills step by step. As interval training, you can repeatedly climb several hills with rest intervals in between. In both cases hill work demands muscle strength as well as stamina from the cardiovascular system without too much stress on the biomechanical system.

Training for reaction speed

Due to the rapidly changing movements in dressage, reaction speed is required. A good example is the work on flying changes at every stride. The horse constantly changes between elasticity and collected maximum strength. This requires a huge amount of strength and muscle coordination. Before a horse is able to jump into the flying changes at every stride, first he has to be guided very carefully into flying changes, then changes with several canter strides in between, and finally the rapid sequence of changes.

A review of the important points:

- Dressage horses should have maximum strength, explosive power, endurance strength and reactive strength.
- Lessons with collection require maximum strength.
- The starting steps to different movements demand explosive power.
- Endurance strength is required for carrying out all dressage movements.
- The most demanding lessons are those that require reactive strength, such as passage, and changing from stride to stride like flying changes.

Tips:

- Take a lot of time for strength training.

- For dressage, all components of strength are necessary. It has been shown that concentrating on improving single moves is the best way to train for strength.

- Figure out your horse's weaknesses. If he has trouble with collection, then he usually needs to work on maximum strength. If he has trouble with increasing speed, then what's lacking is maximum strength and explosive power.

- It's easier to make an assessment of your horse's ability by asking an outside expert to watch. Sometimes an independent trainer can recognize the deficits more quickly.

- When you recognize the weaknesses in your horse's performance, then you can incorporate the specific strength training into your training schedule.

Further references:

Billat VL. 2003. Interval Training for Performance: A Scientific and Empirical Practice. Special Recommendations for Middle and

Long-Distance Running. Part I: Aerobic Interval Training. Sports Med, 31 (1): 13-31.

Zatsiorsky VM. und Kraemer WJ. 2008. Krafttraining. Praxis und Wissenschaft. Meyer und Meyer Verlag, Aachen

Training for speed

Speed is also very important for the dressage horse, whereby there is a general differentiation between reaction speed and speed of movements.

By reaction speed, we mean mainly the reaction of the horse to the rider's aids. The faster the horse is able to react to the rider's aids, the clearer the transitions are between different movements, for example; and the more precisely the movements are carried out. Already in the basic training of the horse, the rider can practice frequent changes of gait: For example, three strides at a walk, three strides at a trot, three at a walk, etc. Later the horse can speed up and slow down many times in the same gait on the long side of the arena. A good way to school the horse's reaction to the rider's sideways driving leg and changing sides to the supporting leg is to have the horse walk, trot and canter on the circle switching from three strides enlarging the circle to three strides reducing the circle.

- **In general, however, the best training for fast, precise reactions to the rider's aids is the consistent adherence to the order "light aids – strong aids – punishment" from the start of any training program. Very soon the horse will learn to react precisely to the lightest aids.**

The breed of the horse largely determines the quickness of movement. Hot-blooded horses frequently show faster movements than calm, warm-blooded horses. Yet even reaction speed can be trained. Calmer horses have a big advantage because they usually have stronger nerves. Nervous thoroughbreds often have the problem of tensing up whenever the rider uses stronger aids, whereas calm warmbloods can be given stronger aids when the rider needs more cooperation without losing their "cool".

In addition to the absolute demand for an immediate reaction to the rider's aids, jumping and cross-country training can also school quickness of movement. As strength increases, the sequence of movements becomes faster and more fluent.

Training for endurance

Frey und Hildenbrand (1994) define stamina in their textbook Introduction to training theories as follows:

"By the word stamina we understand the mental and physical resistance to fatigue demonstrated by athletes. This means the ability to prevent fatigue, to force it out, to keep it at bay during the workout or to decrease it again, and also to be able to recuperate quickly after a workout."

Mental stamina in the cognitive as well as the emotional sector is characterized by the ability to resist a stimulus that is demanding a lessening or a cessation of some kind of stress, and to resist it as long as possible. Even in physical workouts this form of resistance to fatigue plays a major role.

Physical stamina is the resistance to fatigue of the entire organism or individual parts of the system.

The main pillars of endurance are the quality of the transport capacity of the cardiovascular system, the quality of the peripheral oxygen utilization and the metabolic capacity.

All of the factors named by Frey und Hildenbrand (1994) are also valid for equine sports and can be trained extremely well. Even the dressage horse needs a certain amount of stamina, especially when he is going to be used in several dressage tests in one competition. Great stamina is also good for training strength components. A lack of stamina might force training exercises to be suspended too soon. For example, if a horse with poor stamina tires already in the warm-up phase, it won't be possible to continue with systematic strength training afterwards. In this way, stamina is also crucial for training the exercises that require strength. Without it, for example, it would not be possible to practice the collected movements over a longer period of time in order to train intramuscular coordination.

We find the mental stamina required in horses known as performance horses. These horses have the psychological frame of mind willing to go to the limits of their physical capabilities without having to be constantly asked to do so. Otherwise they would refuse to perform at the slightest hint of stress.

There are a number of training methods that can be used to practice endurance. Once more I would like to go into some detail discussing the two most popular training methods: endurance training and interval work.

The methods of endurance training

Generally speaking, this means a training stimulus that continues over a longer period of time at the same level of intensity.

To gauge the intensity of this training stimulus, two measurements are decisive. On the one hand, the amount of lactic acid (lactate) in the venous blood, and on the other hand the measurement of the heart rate during the workout. This training stimulus can be kept at a low level so that the muscle oxygenation is kept constantly in the aerobic zone (at approx. 130 – 140 beats / min). The lactate value should be under 4mmol/ l. If you train in this zone, you will be staying on the safe side, so to speak. Generally, this means you avoid entering the anaerobic zone and sliding into hyperacidity of the muscles. This training zone is highly recommended for weekend athletes and untrained individuals (Marées, 1994 / Frey und Hildenbrand, 1994). In order to build up a foundation for good, aerobic endurance, this is more than adequate.

For competitive athletes in track and field, exercising in a high aerobic / anaerobic transitional zone (ca. 160 - 170 beats / min) is considered the ideal stimulus to train endurance. This is called threshold training. The threshold from aerobic to anaerobic muscle oxygenation can be quite different depending on the individual. Among other things, it depends on the condition and age of the person. If the threshold is a heart rate of about 160 beats / min for an untrained person, for a competitive athlete the heart rate can rise up to 185 beats / min (Marées, 1994 / Frey und Hildenbrand, 1994). However, when threshold training is practiced, there is a danger of hyperacidity in the muscles, which means a blood lactate concentration of over 4mmole/l. In fact, successful results from training can be attained more quickly if you occasionally work out up to the aerobic / anaerobic threshold. Especially with equine training, this cannot be avoided. On the other hand, a heart rate of over 185 beats per minute clearly puts a lot of strain on anaerobic muscle oxygenation. Training regularly at this intensity is contrary to all reason and should not be done.

Ms. Heipertz-Hengst (1999) recommends having a veterinarian determine the individual maximum heart rate of every horse in order to find out the individual aerobic / anaerobic transitional zone. In her experience, the heart rate measured in a horse can be divided up into five large training zones.

She recommends:

"At the beginning of a workout, the equine athlete is exercising mostly in zones 1 to 3, later zones 4 and 5 are included to expand the aerobic capacity and integrate precise training for speed, followed by a cool-down phase in zone 1. There are no simple prescriptions or fixed rules, such as how often or for how long you will have to train in a certain zone in order to reach a certain objective."

	Designation	of the heart % beat max	heart beat/min for your horse	Activity
Z1	Relaxation Recovery	50-60%	115-138	Walk, trot
Z2	Easy exercises	60-70%	139-161	Trot
Z2	Steady-State	70-80%	162-184	Canter
Z4	Anaerobic threshold	80-90%	185-207	Gallopp
Z5	max. capacity	90-100%	208-230	Run

Individual training zones with stress input (Heipertz-Hengst, 1999)

	Categorization	Main purpose	Metabolism	Energy system	Type of twitch muscle fibers
Z1	Very easy	Recuperation; health	Aerobic	Fat	Slow
Z2	Easy	Fitness	Aerobic	Optimal fat burning	Slow
Z2	Moderate to arduous	Performance	Predominantly aerobic	Fats and carbohydrates	Predominantly slow
Z4	Arduous	Improved performance	Mixture of aerobic and anaerobic	Predominantly carbohydrates	Mixture of slow and fast
Z5	Very arduous	Competition (peak performance) form	Rarely aerobic, quite anaerobic	Carbohydrates	Rarely slow, predominantly fast

Large outdoor arenas and racetracks are ideal locations for endurance training. On the racetrack you can start with an even, calm tempo at a canter. After a few training units you should either pick up the pace slowly, or lengthen the stretch of track. If you don't have a racetrack, you can plan to do regular periods of galloping or trot intervals in the outdoor arena, which can be systematically lengthened. It is advisable not to force the horse to gallop at a fast tempo for too long, since riding through the corners at high speeds causes too much stress to the biomechanical system. Trotting and cantering intervals, used as a training stimulus, can be lengthened as well.

It is important both in the outdoor arena as well as on the racetrack that the rider has the feeling that his horse is gradually tiring at a steady pace. If this is not the case, then the rider should increase the pace or select another training method.

Interval training

Interval training in equine sports offers an excellent opportunity to design flexible endurance training. Interval methods can be integrated into training on the racetrack, improving basic rideability, as well as during all forms of dressage work. What characterizes interval training is the constant alternation between work and recovery periods. Recently in track and field sports, the value of interval training as it relates to fundamental aerobic stamina has become a controversial topic once again. A greater and faster increase in performance had been expected from interval training than from endurance training. However, this was not the case. For this reason, some experts writing about training methods have returned to the good, old endurance run (Marées, 1994).

In equine sports interval training is used, for example, on the racetrack by alternating between stretches ridden at a fast pace followed by a rest period ridden at a slow pace.

For dressage training there are ideal opportunities. Sessions alternating between very arduous exercises and the walk – or relaxing rest intervals, can be designed in a variety of ways. Depending on the level of the horse's training, you can practice a new sequence of movements for a few minutes, then have a rest period, then return to practicing the new movements, followed by another break, etc.

The recovery phase between working intervals mustn't last too long. The horse shouldn't completely recover from the workout, otherwise no training stimulus occurs. Little by little the horse will be able to execute the new sequence of movements for a longer period of time and with less fatigue.

The training method "fartlek" in track and field sports is a widely used way of diversifying interval training. Fartlek is the Swedish term for "speed play", and includes a cross-country run with various paces and stresses. In other words, the runner integrates intense sprints into his workout, followed by a recovery run or slow jog slightly below his normal pace. Actually, for the equine athlete, this is none other than hacking through an area as diverse as possible. However, the rider should select an area in advance that corresponds to his horse's condition at the moment. The rider can vary the stretch, for example, by trotting up a hill with a very gradual slope, then cantering up the hill the next time. If the familiar cross-country stretch doesn't require much stamina from the horse anymore, then the rider should consider including steeper hill work or stretches of extended trot. The horse's biomechanical system is challenged in so many different ways on a trail ride that there is a great deal to be gained from it for dressage sports.

While we are on the topic of endurance training, I'd like to bring up the "rewarding rest break" again. Most athletes tend to overdo. Every one of us has had a bad day once in a while, and our equine partners have peaks and valleys as well. A rider with an instinctive feel for his horse will immediately notice that on such days "nothing works". Just go out on the trail with your horse and take a walk. Then you can go back to your training plan the next day. A "lukewarm" day is not going to throw off your training schedule, and it can do a lot for the well being of horse and rider.

A review of the important points:
- Horses need mental and physical endurance.
- Stamina can be improved through endurance or interval training.
- To train stamina, the racetrack, trail riding or the outdoor arena can be used.
- Ten minutes after a workout, a horse in good condition should have values of about 100 hb/min and 16 breaths/min.

Tips:

- **You should not practice endurance training too excessively, since the dressage horse needs to develop strength more.**

- **Endurance training can be useful for the psyche of the horse (mental stamina). Nervous horses are calmed by endurance training, and lazy horses are more willing to work.**

- Long stretches through the woods or in a field are ideal for endurance training, because you can calmly ride your horse forward at a consistent tempo.
- Interval training can easily be integrated into your daily dressage work.
- Don't forget to take rest breaks, otherwise you might start over-training your horse, which can have a detrimental effect.

Further references:

Billat VL. 2003. Interval Training for Performance: A Scientific and Empirical Practice. Special Recommendations for Middleand

Long-Distance Running. Part I: Aerobic Interval Training. Sports Med, 31 (1): 13-31.

Heipertz- Hengst C. (1999) Pferde richtig trainieren. Cadmos, Lüneburg.

Suppleness training

At the end of this chapter I'd like to touch on the subject of suppleness training. Many equestrian athletes use dressage for this very purpose. Correct equine training according to the training scale (see Guidelines for Riding and Driving Vol. 1) is certainly the best suppleness schooling for the horse. Additionally, in recent years several physical therapists have been considering stretching methods for the horse. For performance horses, but also for many backyard horses, these exercises could certainly be of great value in alleviating tense muscles and general physical malaise. However, it is not within the framework of this book to go into these theories, and perhaps also the theories of acupuncture, acupressure and many other methods.

Further references:

Ettl R. 2008. Horse-Agility - Spielerisch und anspruchsvoll trainieren. Müller-Rüschlikon, Stuttgart.

Gösmeier I. 1999. Akupressur für Pferde. Kosmos Verlag, Stuttgart.

Götz C. 2008. Praxishandbuch Freispringen Gymnastik, Training,

Abwechslung. Cadmos Verlag Brunsbeck.

Schmid-Neuhaus A. 2000. Das große Fitnessprogramm für Pferde. Kosmos Verlag, Stuttgart.

Performance check

At the beginning of any training session, trainers and riders should try to make an objective picture of the actual level of the horse's training. The report from the previous owner is not always reliable, especially since you won't get any information about possible gaps in the horse's training. There is a real danger of overwhelming a horse because of a lack of information about his previous training, which could lead to irreparable problems later on. Especially when the rider makes assumptions about what the horse should be able to do, problems can arise if certain steps in the horse's training were neglected or never addressed.

Not only in competitive sports, but also in school athletics and popular sports, "general athletic coordination tests to ascertain whether there are any physical deficiencies" have proven useful (Meyners, 1982). The purpose of these tests is to examine the quality of movement on a regular basis. Using the half-pass as an example, such a test could look like this:

Testing the quality of movements: traversing

- **Phase 1:** Check the lateral bend in the shoulder-in along the rail and on the diagonals. A: walk | B: trot | C: canter
- **Phase 2:** Check the reaction to the sideways driving leg during changes between shoulder-in left and shoulder-in right, for example, riding on the centerline. A: walk | B: trot | C: canter
- **Phase 3:** Check the travers on the long side and the half-pass on the centerline at a walk.
- **Phase 4:** Developing the travers on the long side and half-pass movements on the centerline at a trot and at a canter, still using little bend and collection.
- **Phase 5:** Check the reaction to the rider's aids while doing zigzag half-passes on the centerline at a trot.
- **Phase 6:** Improvement of the bend and collection of travers and half-pass at a trot and at a canter.

The basis of periodic testing is a written account of the exact execution of each element of the movements.
In Phase 1 the written assessment could be:

Take notes on the quality of movement

- **1st Week:** Good reaction to the sideways driving leg, but still escapes with the hindquarters towards the outside. On both sides the contact to the rider's hands is inconsistent.
- **2nd & 3rd Week:** Reaction to the sideways driving leg remains good, however the horse still escapes from the right hand with his hindquarters to the outside, on the left good contact to the rider's hand, on the right still inconsistent.
- **4th Week:** Reaction still good to the sideways driving leg. Good bend on both sides (he no longer escapes to the outside).

A review of the important points:
- Regular, objective assessments of the horse's level of performance is important.
- In order to maintain objectivity, it is advisable to write down the level of performance on a weekly basis.
- Measuring heart rate and breathing help in the assessment of a horse's training level.
- A horse in good condition should show values of 100 beats/min and 16 breaths/min 10 minutes after starting work.

Tips:

- Don't rely on information from the former owner of your horse; there might be huge gaps in his report.

- If you are uncertain about an assessment, have objective experts give you advice. People who train a horse for years are sometimes unable to assess their own horse's strengths and weaknesses.

Further references:

Heipertz- Hengst C (1999) Pferde richtig trainieren. Cadmos, Lüneburg.

With a young horse you will need a few weeks for each phase until the horse is able to execute the sequence of movements correctly. You should go ahead and test horses that are already more advanced phase by phase in the beginning. If there is a deficiency in one of the phases, then it makes sense to stabilize this stage first before continuing with the next phases.

The written account of all of the elements of the movements can be quite instructive at a later date should problems occur. Then you can often read that the horse was having difficulties with the basics of the sequence of movements even at that point. You should go back to that particular phase and practice more until the horse gets it right. Besides, this keeps the rider and trainer from judging a horse's performance based on their own inclinations.

The strength and endurance of a horse are more difficult to assess. Pushy, nervous horses often appear to be fresher than they really are, whereas horses that are too lazy to move may seem to tire quickly, although they might be capable of performing for a longer time. Usually, experienced riders and trainers can sense very quickly when a horse has reached his limits. The rider herself, in fact, has the best feel for the performance capacity of her horse. She is the first one to notice when her mount doesn't react as willingly to her aids, when he constantly tries to elude her or when he doesn't carry out the sequence of movements with his customary animation.

Besides the feeling, measurement of the horse's temperature, pulse and respiration (TPR) is probably the decisive indicator. Take the horse's temperature and if it is over 102.5°F, consult your vet. To measure the heart rate, there are reliable devices that you can tuck under the saddle pad. Respiration can be counted by watching the ribcage and the rise and fall of the flanks. At rest the horse breathes about eight times per minute and has about 40 pulse beats. As already mentioned in Chapter 9, work intervals should have a heart rate of 130 – 140 beats / min, but definitely never more than 160 – 170 beats / min.

Ten minutes after exertion, a horse in good condition should have a heart rate of approximately 100 beats / min and 16 breaths / min. Slight deviations from these values depend on the level of the horse's training and even on the level of excitement. Untrained horses need a bit longer. The better the horse's condition, the sooner he reaches resting TPR. You should be concerned if your horse always seems to be tired or if he takes a very long time to recover from hard exertion. In such cases you should have the horse examined by a veterinarian.

Success in training is manifested by the horse's greater resilience during a workout in which he maintains a steady heart rate, and by his speedy recovery afterwards.

Short comments about doping

Nowadays in modern competitive sports, significantly greater achievements have been made by means of a sound training concept. Yet after years of work, possibly without rest periods for recuperation, the physical limits have been stretched in both man and beast. It's no wonder that trainers are tempted to turn to pharmaceutical solutions to bridge the small gaps in the performance levels of their equine athletes, especially before important competitions. These short-term stopgaps quickly become lasting supports, and before you know it the horse's performance is dependent on the medication he is receiving.

Yet even in competitive sports in the human realm, the question of "success at any price?" is definitely newsworthy (Frey, Hildenbrand, 1994). This makes it all the more important to consider whether we want to give our horses performance-enhancing drugs. Pain is a protective mechanism of the body. It signals that certain structures, or the whole organism, have reached their performance limit. I think it is the duty of the responsible rider also to take his horse's pain seriously. If drugs are used to water down the pain symptoms of the body, it won't be long before the body starts to self-destruct. The resulting damage is often irreparable and the cost is very high: Either the horse will never reach the age at which he is capable of giving his highest performance, or he will have to break off his career prematurely.

In addition, horses that have been drugged endanger not only themselves, but also their riders. Their ability to perceive (for example, the height of a jump or the distance between jumps) and their resilience are so diminished that their reactions are completely unpredictable for the rider.

Training plan
Career path planning

Training plans have to be set up by the rider for each horse individually, with or without the advice of a trainer. Besides the age, the performance potential, the level of training and the sequence of the competitions to be entered, the rider's appointment calendar has to be taken into consideration when drawing up a training plan. Basically, training plans should be made for the long-term. You should be thinking about your horse's career path as soon as possible. Specializing too early, training him too hard and entering him into too many shows in his early years can all lead to premature wear-and-tear and refusals on the part of the horse. Unfortunately, such horses often never reach the age of their highest performance potential.

Basic training should be designed with as much variety as possible. In order to do so, you are encouraged to use as many training tools as possible. The "Old Riding Masters" warned of specializing too early. Even in track and field sports, basic training emphasizes a varied development of strength, endurance, speed and suppleness.

Basic training, conditioning work, and (high performance) competitive training should ideally follow one after the other, allowing a period of two years for each. A good horse can definitely be trained up to the Third (GB: Elementary) Level in all three disciplines, dressage, jumping and eventing, at the same time (Springorum, 1986). In many cases with very good horses, their "true" talent isn't recognized until the transition from the Third Level to the Fourth (GB: Medium) Level. This is where the conditioning work begins. The training intervals become more intensely specialized, the workload is slowly expanded and the number of competitions increases.

After one to two years of schooling, competitive training follows the conditioning work. Not until this stage does it make sense to train the physical performance factors, which would be strength,

endurance, speed and suppleness, specifically for the chosen equine sport (in this case "dressage").

Especially in the sport of dressage, to a certain extent opposing abilities are required. On the one hand, the dressage horse needs strength, stamina, and reaction speed. On the other hand, he also needs a good amount of endurance and, in addition to that, a great deal of suppleness. This is why the variety of the abilities required in this competitive sport determines the diversity of the training.

By the way, the physical fitness of the rider should correspond approximately to that of the horse. A professional rider certainly doesn't have a problem with that. Amateurs, however, and especially those who are seriously involved in their profession, would profit from occasionally thinking about balancing training activities.

A review of the important points:
* The horse's career path should be planned broadly over the long term; specialization should come later.
* A horse's "true" gifts may first appear during the transition from Third to Fourth Level.

Tips:

* **Critically evaluate the "true" aptitude of your horse during the years of her basic training. There is no shame in admitting that you miscalculated the talent of a three-year-old "dressage horse". Many good trainers have had to come to the same conclusion in the past.**

* **The physical talent of a high performance sport horse is not the whole picture: strong nerves are critical as well. Athletic prowess can be misleading. A horse can be a genius in his movements, but this won't help him if he can't cope with the stress of competing. On the other hand, a horse with strong nerves can sometimes compensate for his mediocrity and reach a very high level if he is hardworking and ambitious.**

Annual training plan

Aside from the overriding importance of career path planning, every year differentiated training plans are drawn up. Customarily the year is divided into three periods:

* **Preparation phase**
* **Competition phase**
* **Regeneration phase.**

As a rule, the preparation phase lasts four to six months. During this time all four physical performance factors are worked on, whereby strength and stamina take up the largest amount of time.

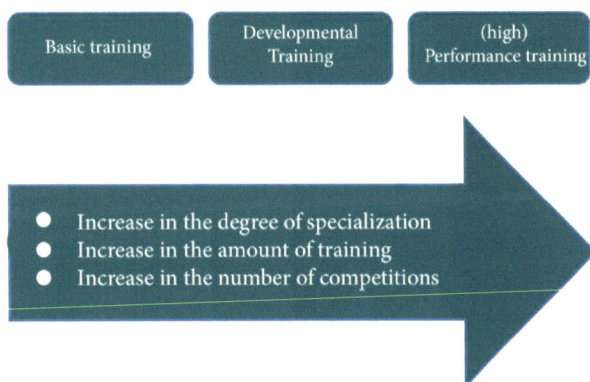

| Basic training | Developmental Training | (high) Performance training |

* Increase in the degree of specialization
* Increase in the amount of training
* Increase in the number of competitions

Figure 17
The long-term training plan
(modified according to G. Frey and E. Hildenbrandt, 1994)

The purpose of the preparation phase is to see to it that at the end of the four to six months, young horses exceed their performance from the previous year, and high performance horses are expected to reach the same level as the year before. However, the intensity of the training should be chosen in such a way that fatigue doesn't set in right before the competition phase starts. To avoid this it is smart to plan in a couple of days of rest every four weeks.

Not until the competition period do we strive for peak physical and mental fitness. We recommend reducing strength and endurance training during this time and concentrating more on intramuscular coordination and suppleness, as the competitions themselves are very exhausting for the horse. As a rule, two to three performance peaks should be planned into the horse's training schedule at the most. Often these are determined by the show circuit. But sometimes you are also in the position to choose among the most important competitions. Of course, the best-case scenario would be to have the three fitness peaks evenly distributed across the competition period. Regenerative phases between the three fitness peaks help to safeguard the horse's vitality and health throughout the entire show season.

It's not just event horses or the jumpers that require a phase of physical and especially mental regeneration at the end of every competitive year, but also dressage horses. After the last show the training program should be reduced slowly, however. The organism of a high performance horse grows accustomed to the stress during the intensive competition phase. If you reduce the training too quickly, the horse might react by having problems with his metabolism and especially with his cardiovascular system. It takes two to three weeks for the cardiovascular and digestive systems to adjust to easy workouts. This easy training can consist of trail riding and regular relaxation exercises and should be maintained for several weeks. Experience has shown that horses with "active" rather than "passive" rest intervals start off the new show season with a more positive attitude.

It becomes challenging when a horse competes both in the outdoor and indoor riding seasons. This is when the instinctive feel that rider and trainer have for the horse must come into play. In order to avoid injuries and demotivation caused by too much stress, any indications of over-training such as sleep disorders, lack of appetite, loss of weight and a rise in the resting pulse rate should be addressed immediately by shifting to a regeneration phase to allow the horse time to recover.

In the Appendix there is an example of an annual plan for a Fourth to a Grand Prix (GB: Advanced) Level dressage horse competing in the outdoor season. Attached to the annual plan are weekly plans for a typical week in the conditioning phase, in the breaks between shows and a suggestion for designing a week of competition. However, these plans are not for copying. They should serve as motivation for you to design an individual training plan of your own.

A Review of the important points:

- Divide your year up into a preparatory phase, competitive phase and regenerative phase.
- When horses are being used in the outdoor season as well as the indoor season, it is the rider's responsibility to plan a period of regeneration into the schedule occasionally, so that the horse doesn't get hopelessly burned out at some point

Tips:

- As a rule of thumb, there should be two to three periods of peak performance during the competitive phase.
- Decide at the beginning of the year which of the important "large" competitions you would like to ride in, and then plan to participate in smaller shows before these important competitions take place, leaving two weeks between each competition.
- • If your horse seems to be having fitness problems during the season, it's better to omit one of the competitions than to push him beyond his limit.

Special aspects of the training theories for dressage horses at the Third to Fourth Levels

Relaxation

Relaxation exercises play a large role in the training of all horses, and even for high performance dressage horses competing at the Grand Prix Level. For the latter group, however, the relaxation phase at the beginning of the workout should be significantly shortened, in contrast to the work with young horses, even though these exercises are still necessary.

The relaxation phase can be compared to the warm-up phase of track-and-field athletes. It prepares the organism for a workout. During this phase the catabolism swings to an aerobic / anaerobic equilibrium on the performance level, and the cardiovascular system is increasingly stimulated. As a result, there is an increase in the blood supplied to the entire biomechanical system and the organism can begin working without damaging itself.

Relaxation phases are necessary again and again between individual work sessions, although here they serve a different purpose. They give the organism an opportunity to refill its reserves of phosphorus and carry away intermediate catabolic products. Rest intervals also contribute to mental relaxation following the previous tension during the workout. After an beneficial relaxation break, the horse will be ready to work again, as long as he isn't exhausted already.

On the days the horse has off, moderate, relaxing dressage work helps the horse recuperate quickly. The blood supply to the organism increases and intermediate catabolic products from previous workouts can be broken down more quickly

Extensions

The extensions at a trot, canter and to a certain extent also at a walk depend first and foremost on the horse's strength. What is required is impulsion: both normal impulsion as well as endurance impulsion. To do this, muscle groups are required primarily to stretch the joints. This is a contrast to collection, whose main feature is to hold the horse's body weight at an angle over the hind legs.

For this reason it's a good idea to switch between exercises with extensions and exercises with collection, because the muscle groups used in extensions can rest during the collection work, and vice versa.

Figure 18 - Horse at a working trot in the relaxation phase

Common methods for working with extensions in dressage training are addressed briefly in the following:

- **The most elegant way to practice extensions can be done with horses that readily work in collection. In collection the body's center of gravity is shifted to the hindquarters while the shoulders are noticeably released. If you now increase the pace from the collection for a few strides, the thrust comes from the hindquarters. The forehand can move more freely and expansively because much of the horse's weight has been shifted to the hindquarters. Initially, after a few strides the horse will shift his weight back to the forehand. The rider should only increase the pace for a few strides until the horse has gained in strength, then he can ask the horse for more strides at a**

Figure 19 - Another horse at a working trot in the relaxation phase. The horse is chewing long and low. The horse "chews the reins out of the rider's hands", which helps, on the one hand, in the relaxation phase, and on the other hand it is a good test of the suppleness of the horse during dressage training.

brisker pace. This method is definitely the most gentle for the forehand, but there is one disadvantage: an advanced stage of training is the prerequisite.

- **Extensions ridden on large, curved lines (for example, a circle with a diameter of 30 meters (90 ft.))**

  * For some horses it is easier to encourage an energetic stride by working with one hind leg at a time. This is best accomplished on a curved line. In the beginning a tilted position of the legs will be noticeable, in addition to the unavoidable pressure on the forehand.

- **Riding extensions (mostly at a trot) the length of a large outdoor or indoor riding arena (at least 25 m (75 ft.) x 50 m (150 ft.)**

  * Some horses start to extend their strides powerfully when they notice how uncomfortable it is to move on the forehand for longer periods of time. This method has the same disadvantage as riding extensions on the circle.

- **Training extensions in series**

  * For example, increase the pace 4 x 1 long side, take a break afterwards, then increase the pace again 4 x 1 long side, etc. Besides training impulsion, the rideability of the horse can be improved by repetitions at a brisk pace followed by a slow one. This method is recommended for horses that do extensions easily, however.

Flying changes

Training flying changes basically requires reaction speed and speed of movement from the horse.

Frey and Hildenbrand (1994) write about training for speed as follows:

Neuromuscular control processes determine elementary speed; speed in the complex coordination required for competitive sports is essentially determined by strength and the elasticity of the musculature as well as intramuscular coordination. It includes both the components reaction speed and speed of movement. We differentiate between simple reactions and selective reactions, cyclical and acyclical action speed and speed strength. The cyclical speed of movement is the individual, optimal product consisting of the amplitude and frequency of movement. The amplitude of movement appears to be significant especially at a low level of performance, and systematic strength training is particularly rewarding for this level.

At the beginning of schooling, while learning flying changes at every stride, reaction speed is in the foreground. A precise execution of the flying change, exactly at the right point, depends on the quick reaction to fine aids from the rider, and the strength to complete a sequence of movements.

Though reaction speed is, to a great extent, an innate ability, it can be increased by 10 to 20 percent through training. The reaction time, ability to focus and the reliability of the reaction can be improved while training the flying change at every stride as a simple reaction time combined with systematic strength training.

The following methods can help in the training of flying changes:

Strength training
- General basic training
- Varied cross-country trails with hill work
- Jumping single fences and combinations at a trot

Training reaction speed:
- Consistent adherence to the sequence: "light aids – strong aids – punishment"
- Demand immediate reaction to the rider's aids
- Exercises (such as transitions) practiced with short time intervals in between
- Switching to learning the sequence of movements by riding at a free pace first (strength for collected change has not been trained yet)
- Ride the flying change with a light seat over the jumps or between the jumps.

The closer together the sequence is in which the horse learns to jump into the flying change, the more strength and speed of movement are required. At first he needs strength in general, then later reactive strength for the speed of movement and strength endurance in his collection for jumping the tempi changes.

The correct straightness of the horse is useful when it comes to tempi changes. It not only makes it possible for a skillful execution of the sequence of movements, but also the even distribution of pressure on both hind legs. What counts here is more the optimization of the level of strength rather than the maximization of it, which will be accomplished to a large extent by means of improved intramuscular coordination.

Allowing your horse to spend time in the pasture is an important plus in his conditioning training and increases his willingness to work

An improvement of technique and the maximum frequency of movement are just as important as an increase of strength. The following points can lead to this improvement:

Conditioning work:
- General strength training like for reaction speed
- Dressage training with work on maintaining collection
- Cross-country training with extended hill work
- Jumping practice chiefly from the trot

Training techniques:
- Refinement of the rider's aids
- Demand the flying change from a collected canter
- Riding the flying change at every stride in different situations (while jumping, on the trail, on different footing, on a curved line, etc.)

Training the frequency of movement:
- Demand transitions at a high rate of frequency (for example, three strides at a walk, three strides at a canter, three at a walk, etc.)
- Gradual increase in the frequency of tempi changes (tempi changes á 6 strides, up to every stride)
- Training tempi changes in series, for example:
  * Series [1]: Change the pace four times on the long side of the arena
  * Break: [10-15] minutes
  * Series [2]: Same as series [1]
  * Break: [10-15] minutes
  * Series [3]: Same as series [1]

Half-passes

The basis for correct half-passes, whether at a trot or a canter, is endurance strength for collection and suppleness. Compared to other lessons that require similar abilities, for training half-passes the sideways tilted position of the legs should be taken into account. This puts a strain not only on the tendons and ligaments of untrained horses, but also in large measure on the joints. A significant amount of pressure is exerted selectively, one-sidedly and increasingly at faster paces on the side surfaces of the cartilage. A large part of this pressure is on the forehand during the half-pass movements, which are ridden without collection. The more the horse's center of gravity is distributed on all four legs during collection, the more evenly the pressure is exerted on the legs during half-passes.

The best way to prepare the horse's biomechanical system for this special pressure is to take him out trail riding.

If you consciously have the horse take the diagonal across a slope once in a while, you are preparing him for similar pressure on his legs during half-pass exercises. But be careful! This training also has to be given in small doses. Horses that are used to moving on even footing can easily come down with a stretched ligament. Bit by bit every horse will become more sure-footed and be able to canter across the hills for longer periods without injuring himself.

The strength training for half-passes corresponds to that required by the collected lessons (see Piaffe), which is why it isn't necessary to go over this topic again. However, there are specific features of suppleness training for half-passes.

Figure 22 - Half-passes to the left. The tilted position of the legs is quite noticeable in the half-pass, which puts uneven pressure on tendons, ligaments and joints.

Figure 23 - A similar pressure is exerted on the horse's limbs while crossing the slope, similar to in the half-pass in Figure 22.

After a period of suppleness training, the horse will need a rest break. Practicing the half-passes at a walk can be neatly included as a part of the relaxation phase. It makes sense to switch back and forth between work on the lateral movements and "chewing the reins out of the rider's hands" in all three gaits.

Good exercises are as follows:
- Riding travers and half-pass at a walk. When that seems to be under control, start trying it at a trot and a canter.
- Frequent switching of leads and directions, for example, riding a zigzag half-pass promotes suppleness in the horse and obedience to the rider's aids
- Travers and half-passes can be combined with other lateral movements, for example, about turns left or right – half-pass / shoulder-in – half-pass, etc. Here, too, suppleness is practiced. And as a by-product you are fine-tuning the rider aids.

Piaffe

Piaffe, or riding a collected, elevated trot on the spot, is the most collected of all the dressage movements. Its execution requires mostly strength from the horse, and, if it is practiced over a longer period of time, endurance strength. The biggest challenge in reference to the catabolism of the muscle is learning to do the piaffe. In the beginning the horse's strength / endurance is not sufficient to develop an aerobic / anaerobic steady state. For this reason the piaffe is mainly performed in the anaerobic zone in the initial stages. Very soon the results are a high blood lactate concentration and the fatigue of the musculature that accompanies it. When the horse has developed the necessary intramuscular coordination through successful training, as well as the necessary endurance strength, then he can perform the piaffe over a longer period of time without tiring.

However, there is a solution for the challenges associated with learning to do the piaffe. For generations in practice, the piaffe has been started with half steps, which corresponds to the demand for only a single piaffe step from a diagonal pair of legs. From the perspective of sports theory, this makes good sense. In fact, if you demand exertion for 2 – 4 seconds, then the muscle's energy requirements can be covered by the existing reserves of phosphorus in the form of creatine phosphate. If you give the organism a few minutes' rest afterwards, the energy reserves can be refilled. In this way the muscle doesn't even reach the anaerobic zone, and the danger of hyperacidity of the musculature is banished.

Figure 20 - Performance of the piaffe on the double lunge line by a horse with relatively little training

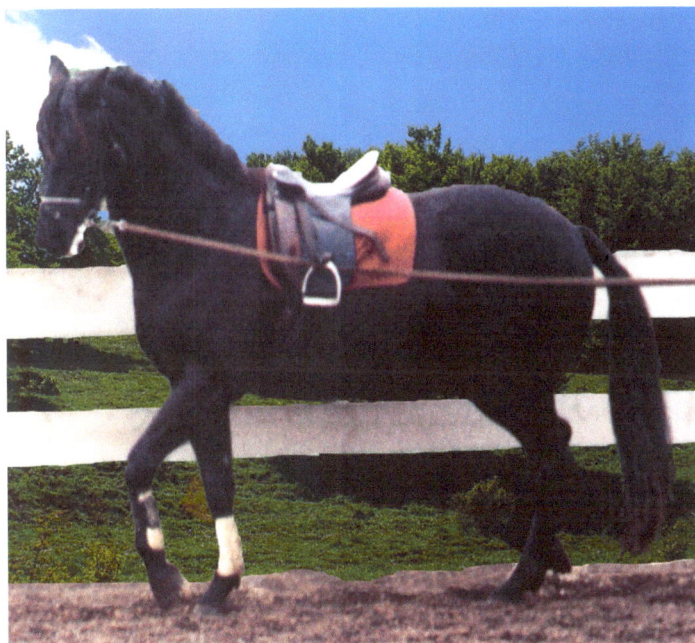

Figure 21 - In an attempt to demonstrate the bend at the haunches, the horse loses his strength. He escapes to the side with his hindquarters instead of trying to get under the center of gravity.

Essentially, intramuscular coordination is being improved whenever there are short phases in which enormous bursts of strength are required. With sufficiently long rest periods, you can practice the piaffe with your horse several times in an hour. Muscle coordination will improve visibly, and thus one of the cornerstones for developing strength will be established.

Gradually the horse will be capable of accomplishing full steps, and later a series of rhythmic, elevated piaffe steps. Now the organism is able to cover its energy requirements aerobically. There are hardly any traces of lactic acid even after long periods of performing the piaffe.

Doing a lot of hill work out on the trail is a good way to support the strength training necessary for the collected movements in dressage. Cross-country training using the fartleks method is also an excellent way to enhance your conditioning work.

At the very beginning of the piaffe movements, training the horse in hand has proven to be quite useful. Half steps in hand don't require the same amount of strength as they would with a rider, as the horse does not have to balance the rider's weight along with his own. Practicing the piaffe in hand at first with many steps and then afterwards under the rider should be done with half steps to begin with. On the other hand, the horse can be schooled simultaneously both in hand and with the rider.

Passage

The passage, or exaggerated trot, requires reactive strength from the horse. This type of strength was manifested in training theories only recently (Frey und Hildenbrand, 1994). In the case of the passage, the horse constantly switches between exertion in the collected position and impulsion. This is precisely what characterizes reactive strength according to training theories: the ability to switch from powerfully holding the body weight to forward thrust as quickly as possible and without tiring. Today it is assumed that it is a self-contained form of strength. This would explain why horses that readily go into a collected position are not necessarily able to do the passage. On the other hand, there are young horses that go into strides similar to the passage at the slightest sign of excitement, although they are unfamiliar with collection.

It is too tempting to ride the passage on young horses that naturally show a display of dominance. Yet most young horses are unable to go into collected gaits with the correct bend of the haunches. Riding the passage too often at this stage can easily lead to overburdening and wear-and-tear of the hocks.

In order to train reactive strength, it makes sense to combine impulsion (see Extensions) and the endurance strength of collection (see Piaffe). For horses that naturally have a suspended trot, the passage can be developed from the collected trot very easily. Horses that are readily collected and have a great deal of strength, but not that much elasticity, can more easily be trained to do the passage from the piaffe by having them step powerfully out of the piaffe, but still using the seat and back aids to maintain collection.

As always, training of the passage should also be accomplished in small doses in order to avoid overstraining the biomechanical structures necessary for reactive strength.

Glossary

Classical equestrian schooling / The art of riding

This refers to the traditional equestrian schooling or art of riding as represented by the Spanish Riding School in Vienna or the German Calvary School in Hanover, for example. We reject emphatically any haphazard, hurried approach to equine training that subjects the horse to painful procedures in the name of "classical dressage". These methods omit stages in the horse's training that are vital to his mental and physical well-being.

Riding in position

Riding in position refers to the Classical equestrian schooling for the lesson "shoulder-fore". As many dressage riders certainly already know, this is the first step before mastering the "shoulder-in". When doing the shoulder-fore exercise, the whole horse is one step away from bending around the rider's inner leg. When observing from the front, the horse's outside foreleg is not stepping exactly in front of the inner hind leg like in the shoulder-in exercise, but it is stepping between the hind legs. This used to be called riding in position. Many modern riding books refer to "riding in position" when they mean using the reins to put the horse's neck on the inside or the outside even on a straight line.

Bend of the haunches

This is the angle of the upper joints of the hindquarters, namely the joints of the hip, knee and hock during correct collection. A bend of the hindquarters that only involves the hock and not the haunches can be observed frequently in untrained or overstrained horses.

Flying change at every stride

This is the flying change from one canter stride to the next canter stride, also called one-tempi changes.

Tempi changes

This signifies the change of leads in a sequence with defined distance; for example, every 6 canter strides or every 5 canter strides all the way to changes at every stride (flying change at every stride).

Enlarging and reducing the circle

This is an excellent exercise and can be ridden in every gait. It is important that the horse remains bent in the direction of the movement on the circular path. Pressure from the inside leg enlarges the circle, while giving steady pressure with the outside leg reduces the circle. The exercise becomes more difficult at the higher gaits and when the circle is reduced or enlarged very quickly. Nervous horses have a tendency to bolt at the canter when they feel the sideways pressure. If this should happen, the rider should make every effort to react consistently to the bolting, first with the seat and back aids, and then with full halts. The goal of the exercise is for the horse to willingly follow the pressure of the legs on the curved line without the rider having to use the reins to guide him. When this goal is reached, then enlarging and reducing the circle is good for all horses to practice obedience to leg pressure and the quickness of reactions. We have used this exercise at shows before jumping an obstacle course to check the rideability of the horse once more shortly before the test.

"Chewing the reins out of the rider's hand"

On the one hand, this is one of the required exercises in the Second Level test (GB: Novice), on the other hand this is an absolute "must" for all horses at all levels of training and for all types of riding. In this exercise the horse is supposed to stretch his head long and low after a workout. The horse's withers are the highest point in this case. At the same time the horse should not alter his center of gravity, his rhythm or his pace.

Letting the horse chew the reins out of the rider's hand (giving the reins completely) is a good way to check relaxation and the real contact to the rider's aids. It should be possible to do this exercise correctly at any time during the relaxation phase. If this is not the case, then there should be a short rest period during the workout. Additionally this exercise is very good for the horse as far as his elasticity, relaxation and recovery are concerned. At all levels of training, "chewing the reins out of the rider's hands" offers horses a regeneration phase between exhausting work sessions.

Bibliography

Brügger, A. Die Erkrankungen des Bewegungsapparates und seines Nervensystems. (Stuttgart: Gustav Fischer, 1980).

Brügger, A. Gesunde Körperhaltung im Alltag. (Zürich: Dr. A. Brügger, 1980).

Cannon, W.B. The wisdom of the body. (New York: Norton, 1932).

Darwin, Charles. The foundation of the origin of species. (London: Cambridge University Press, 1842).

Diacont, A. and Loeffler, A. Richtiges Training – Gesundes Pferd: Anatomisches Grundwissen fuer Reiter und Ausbilder. (Stuttgart: Rueschlikon, 2006).

Miesner S, Putz M, and Plewa M., Deutsche Reiterliche Vereinigung e.V.(FN), Richtlinien für Reiten und Fahren – Band 1. (Warendorf: Fn-Verlag, 2005, 2013).

Ettl, Renate. Pferde gut in Form – Richtiges Training fuer Fitness und Gesundheit. (Stuttgart: Rueschlikon, 2007)

Ettl, Renate. Horse Agility - Spielerisch und anspruchsvoll trainieren. (Stuttgart: Mueller-Rueschlikon, 2008)

Frey G and Hildenbrandt E. Einführung in die Trainingslehre 1. Grundlagen. (Schorndorf: Hofmann, 1994).

Heipertz- Hengst, C. Pferde richtig trainieren. (Lüneburg: Cadmos, 1999).

Ivers, T. The Fit Racehorse. (Cincinnati, OH, Esprit Racing Team).

Karl von, P. Irrwege der modernen Dressur. Die Suche nach der "klassischen" Alternative. 978-3861274131 (Brunsbek, 2006).

Karstens, H. (1980) Das Military Pferd.

Klimke, R. Military. Geschichte, Training, Wettkampf. (Stuttgart: Franckh, 1967).

Lamarck, J-B. Zoologische Philosophie, Mit Einleitung und Anhang: Das phylogenetische System der Tiere nach Haeckel. (Leipzig: Kröner, 1909).

Leng, V. Das Vielseitigkeitspferd. Der Vielseitigkeitsreiter. Ausbildung, Training, Event. Blv (München: Verlagsgesellschaft, 1992).

List, M. Physiotherapeutische Behandlung der Traumatologie. (Heidelberg: Springer Verlag, 2004).

Marees de, H. Sportphysiologie. (Köln: Tropon)

Markworth, P. Sportmedizin: Physiologische Grundlagen. (Reinbek: Rowohlt, 1983)

Meyners, E. Lernen nach dem Regelkreismodell. Sportlehre für Reiten.Fahren. Voltigieren. (Warendorf: FN-Verlag, 1982) pp 21–36.

Müller-Wohlfahrt, H.W. and Kübler, U. Hundert Prozent fit und gesund. Das Geheimnis des gesunden Menschen. (München: Heyne, 1998).

Oese, E. and A. Pferdesport – Ein Handbuch für Trainer, Übungsleiter, Pferdezüchter und Aktive. (Berlin: Sportverlag, 1982).

Opitz, G. 'Der Muskelschmerz', Schmerz und Akupunktur 3 (2005), 151-163.

Pikhala, L. (1930) Allgemeine Richtlinien für das athletische Training. In: Krümel C (ed) Athletik. Ein Handbuch der lebenswichtigen Leibesübungen. (München: Lehmann, 1930) pp 185-.

Scheunert, A. and Trautmann, A. Lehrbuch der Veterinär-Physiologie. (Berlin: Parey,1987)

Schönfelder, W.D. 'Wertschätzung"– Voraussetzung für erzieherisches Verhalten im Voltigier- und Reitunterricht'. Sportlehre für Reiten. Fahren. Voltigieren. (Warendorf: FN-Verlag, 1982) pp 51–60.

Springorum, B. Hinweise zum Konditionstraining der Military-Pferde. (Warendorf: FN-Verlag, 1986)

Stashak T.S. and Wissdorf, H. Adams' Lahmheit bei Pferden. (Hannover, Schaper M. & H, 2007)

Steinbrecht, G. Das Gymnasium des Pferdes. (Berlin: Richard Schröder, 1935).

Steiner, M. 'Biomechanics of tendon healing', (J Biomech 15, 1982) pp 951–958.

Sturm, P. 'Brauchen wir Training und Wettkampf?' Athletik – Jahrbuch 1914. (Berlin: Selbstverlag der Deutschen Sport-Behörde für Athletik, 1914).

Umminger, W. Helden, Götter, Übermenschen : Eine Kulturgeschichte menschl. Höchstleistungen. (Düsseldorf: Econ-Verlag, 1962).

Training Schedule

Month	Week	Competitions	Period	Training
January	1		Period of development - Working on the basics - Increased strength and stamina training	Training: once a day, more comprehensive than in the regenerative phase; work once a week to the limit of the horse's ability. Training goal: improvement of contact and stamina. Dressage work, training on the trail at a trot and climbing hills. Once a week jumping, longeing and in-hand work
	2			
	3			
	4			Break: suppleness work, walking on the trail with climbing, longeing
February	1			Training: twice a week, twice a day, otherwise once a day – twice a week to the limit of the horse's ability. Training goal: improvement of impulsion and stamina. Dressage work at a free pace, training on the trail with longer stretches at a trot, Hill climbing the same as the previous week, jumping: mainly for stretching, longeing
	2			
	3			
	4			Break: suppleness work, walking on the trail with climbing, longeing
March	1			Training: 4 times a week, twice daily, otherwise once a day – three times a week to the limit of the horse's ability. Training goal: improvement of straightness, strength and stamina. Dressage work: lateral work and movements in collection, in-hand work with different movements, training on the trail: lengthen the hill climbing, racetrack also at a gallop jumping: from the trot and higher jumps
	2			
	3			
	4			Break: suppleness work, walking on the trail with long stretches of climbing, longeing
April	1			Training; 5 times a week twice a day, otherwise once a day three times a week to the limit of the horse's ability. Training goal: improvement of collection, strength and stamina. Dressage work: lateral work and movements in collection, strengthening, training on the trail: mainly climbing, in-hand work with movements in collection, jumping; from the trot
	2			
	3			
	4			Break: twice a day easy dressage work, jumping, trail riding, longeing
May	1	Preliminary competition	1. Period of peak performance / Period of peak performance from May to October Text see next page	Training: twice a day except Thurs. / Fri. once a week to the limit of the horse's ability. Training goal: to maintain condition and strength - improve intramuscular coordination and flexibility. Dressage work: improve movements, in-hand work with transitions and movements, training on the trail: riding at a walk and one part hill climbing, jumping; once a week jumps or cavalettis
	2	Preliminary competition		
	3	Preliminary competition		
	4			Break: twice a day easy dressage work, jumping, trail riding, longeing
June	1	Preliminary competition		The same as before the break
	2			
	3	Larger competition i.e., qualification for championship		
	4			Break: once a day easy dressage work, jumping, trail riding, longeing

42

Training Schedule

Month	Week	Period	Competitions	Phase	Training
July	1			Period of peak performance from May to October - Improvement of the movements - Maintenance of stamina and strength - Work on flexibility and intramuscular coordination	
July	2	2. Period of peak performance	Preliminary competition		
July	3				The same as in the previous section
July	4		Preliminary competition		
August	1				
August	2				
August	3		Larger competition		Break: once a day easy dressage work, jumping, trail riding, longeing
August	4				Break: twice a day suppleness work, trail riding at a walk, longeing
September	1	3. Period of peak performance			Training: twice a day three times a week to the limit of the horse's ability Training goal: correction of the mistakes made in previous competitions Riding the movements / rideability / racetrack / in-hand work / jumping / trail with 3 parts climbing
September	2				
September	3		Preliminary competition		The same as in the previous section
September	4				
October	1		Preliminary competition		
October	2				Break: once a day easy dressage work, jumping, trail riding, longeing
October	3				The same as in the previous section
October	4		Larger competition Possibly championship		
November	1			Active regeneration phase	Reduction in training: transition from twice a day to once a day No longer use stressful training such as the racetrack or excessive dressage training and jumping.
November	2				
November	3				
November	4				
December	1				Maintenance of the horse's basic condition, rhythm and suppleness Once a day diversified work Relaxing work, trail riding at a walk, free jumping, longeing
December	2				
December	3				
December	4				

Example of a weekly plan – competition week	
Monday	Morning: Dressage training – Improvement of basic rideability; correction of one or two movements Afternoon: Trail riding at a walk
Tuesday	Morning: Trail riding - 2-3 parts hill climbing, longer stretches at a quiet trot Afternoon: relaxing work
Wednesday	Morning: Dressage training – Repitition of the corrections done on Monday Afternoon: Longe with possibly some in-hand work
Thursday	Easy work - Trail riding at a walk or relaxing dressage work Possible trip to competition venue – relaxing work on the premises
Friday	Competition
Saturday	Competition
Sunday	Competition

Example of a weekly plan – developmental training; Training goal: collection, strength, stamina	
Monday	Morning: Dressage training – Movements in collection to the limit of the horse's ability Afternoon: Longe
Tuesday	Morning: trail riding – one part hill climbing Afternoon: relaxing work
Wednesday	Trail riding at a walk without any pressure
Thursday	Morning: continuation of the dressage work from Monday to the limit of the horse's ability Afternoon: trail riding at a walk
Friday	Morning: jumping – series of jumps + jumps from the trot Afternoon: longe with in-hand work
Saturday	Morning: dressage work – work on basic rideability Afternoon: race track at a quiet canter and accelerate the pace for approx. 400m
Sunday	Free jumping or longe

Example of a weekly plan – break in competition; training once a day	
Monday	Relaxing dressage work
Tuesday	Trail riding at a walk
Wednesday	Cavaletti work or free jumping
Thursday	Trail riding at a walk
Friday	Relaxing dressage work
Saturday	Race track at a quiet trot + canter, do not go to the limit of the horse's ability
Sunday	Longe

www.ingramcontent.com/pod-product-compliance
Lightning Source LLC
LaVergne TN
LVHW072108070426
835509LV00002B/64

* 9 7 8 3 9 8 0 8 1 3 4 6 4 *